A Search for Meaning in Love, Sex, and Marriage

Revised Edition

A Search for Meaning in Love, Sex, and Marriage

by
Hugo L. Hurst, CFX

Saint Mary's Press
Christian Brothers Publications
Winona, Minnesota

Imprimi Potest: Philip L. Dougherty, C.F.X.
                 Provincial
                 July 18, 1975

Nihil Obstat: Joseph M. McGee
                 Censor Librorum *ad hoc*
                 July 18, 1975

Imprimatur: †Thomas J. McDonough
                 Archbishop of Louisville
                 July 18, 1975

The nihil obstat and imprimatur are official declarations that a book or pamphlet is free of doctrinal error. No implication is contained therein that those who have granted the nihil obstat and imprimatur agree with the contents, opinions, or statements expressed.

Fourteenth Printing—July 1980

Cover design by R.G. Davis

ISBN: 0-88489-063-5

Library of Congress Card Catalog Number: 75-9961

Copyright 1975 by St. Mary's College Press,
Terrace Heights, Winona, Minnesota 55987

Contents

Foreword 7

Preface 9

What Is The Meaning of Love?

1. Love: A Discussion of the Question 15
2. What Are People's Attitudes Toward Love? 17
3. Love Considered as Union 23
4. A Definition and Description of Love 43
5. Christian Love—What Is It? 63
6. Love: Some Conclusions 71

Bibliography 73

What Meaning Exists In Sex and Sexuality?

7. Sex: A Discussion of the Question 77
8. Instincts in Man: A Positive Good 79
9. Sex and Sexuality: Human Meanings and Implications 87
10. The Function of the Sex Organs 97
11. Sex and Morality 111
12. Obstacles to Growth and Maturity 123

13	Sex: Some Conclusions	159
Bibliography		161

What Is Marriage for People Today?

14	Marriage: A Discussion of the Question	167
15	What Is Marriage?	171
16	How Can A Person Best Prepare for Marriage?	181
17	Factors Contributing to a Successful Marriage	193
18	Factors Possibly Destructive of Marriage	215
19	Marriage: Some Conclusions	231
Bibliography		233

Foreword

Love, sex, and marriage have been an area of wilderness and upheaval for a generation.

Values which have guided people in this area for centuries are being questioned, with accompanying changes in (1) the attitude toward women, (2) the attitude toward sexual activity, and (3) the attitude toward marriage.

The universal attitude toward women until quite recently was that women were property. Legal codes of states and churches have been based on this attitude. A woman belongs to her husband, her husband is responsible for her debts, her husband has to provide for her. Attitudes toward sexual activity have tended to restrict sexual activity to a technique for producing children. Throughout the world marriage has been based on property laws. Both states and churches have approached marriage from the viewpoint of a legal contract. Marriage has been formulated as an exchange of bodies, rights, and obligations, with an unequal distribution of both rights and obligations to the male.

Women, at least a considerable number of women, are insisting on more equal status before the law and also in interpersonal relationships. At present an amendment to the Constitution of the United States intended to affirm that women have equal rights with men is in the process of ratification by the states. New ideas about women are already generating a new set of values in love, sex, and marriage. This book, though not directly concerned with feminist issues, assumes for women equality with men as human persons.

There are three approaches to these changing values about love, sex, and marriage. The first is to keep on affirming the traditional beliefs about women and so maintain the traditional values. Some states, some churches, and some individuals have leaned toward this approach. The second possibility is to set the traditional beliefs and values aside and start constructing new beliefs and values based on new ideas about women and their relationships to men. Some states, some churches, and some individuals are going this route. A third possibility is to hold on to as much of the old beliefs and values as seems to be solid while reaching out for as much of the new as seems necessary to correspond to the growth of human consciousness. *A Search for Meaning in Love, Sex, and Marriage* takes this third approach.

This approach will not satisfy everybody. The traditionalist will feel that it has given too much attention to the new ideas and values. The revolutionary will feel that it holds on to the traditional views too much. Even the moderate who generally is open both to the new and to the old will be unhappy at moments, for he or she will not always agree with the exact position where the author takes his stand.

However, it is not necessary for the reader to agree with the author all the time. Maybe it would help every young person, parent, teacher, and clergyman who reads this book if every page were stamped: *Not written by God*. Then the reader could proceed sensibly; for then he or she could use this book as a religion book should be used, namely, as a stimulus to help the reader define beliefs and values which will enable one to understand and deepen his or her own experience as a follower of Jesus the Christ.

This book is a challenge.

Andrew Panzarella, FSC

Preface

Taking the cue from Viktor Frankl in his book, *Man's Search for Meaning*, this book is a search for meaning in three important areas of life — love, sex, and marriage. Even more, it is a challenge to proficiency techniques, the how-to and cookbook approaches to love, sex, and marriage that flood the market. The impression left by many of these manuals is that if readers follow the prescribed directions, use the proper techniques and suggested gimmicks, they will arrive at instant happiness and fulfillment. The first lesson that the young who are looking for meaning in love, sex, and marriage must learn is that no amount of expertise in what should or should not be done in a given situation will ever create success in these areas of life.

Today's youth are constantly bombarded with varied and contradictory opinions and theories about love, sex, and marriage. Adolescents are exposed to every conceivable point of view from parents, friends, teachers, books, magazines, and the communications media. There is no end of rationale for this or that custom, point of view, value, or practice. It is no wonder that the young tend to lose their footing in this swamp of contradiction and confusion.

Young people who are honest with themselves admit to searching for a way of life that has meaning and value. Unfortunately, our modern society too often sets them up as clay pigeons for everything that is new and different. There is much talk about the romantic ideal of love, premarital sex with love in a meaningful relationship, permissiveness with affection, open marriage, and a hedonistic view of life with emphasis on fun now. The relationship between men and women is undergoing radical changes — and we are just at the beginning. Traditional roles of male and female in society are fast fading.

This is but a partial list of the difficulties that youth must face in their search for values that will guide their decisions. The real problem is: Has our society prepared the young to make decisions in these changing times? Because of the implications for each person's future peace, happiness, and fulfillment, these decisions are not to be made lightly.

This book was written to help young men and women search for meaning and value in love, sex, and marriage and to help them make decisions about life as thinking, caring human beings. By means of criticism and evaluation, the book attempts to open up a path to value and meaning. The basic thesis of the book is that every person is an individual, different from all others, and not a thing or a commodity. A person is not a unit of mass production, a thing to be used, but rather a unique creation with a body-spirit that expresses all that he is, all that he can and ought to be as a human being. Each woman or man is distinguishable from the "average," "normal" woman or man because no one else has the physical-psychic-spiritual makeup that she or he possesses. This is the value and dignity of every human being.

On the basis of the above assumption, this book attempts to search for values with the individual *as a person* on the center stage. There is only one real way that leads to personal peace, joy, happiness, and fulfillment — and that is the way of love. But no matter what personal relationships we have with others, we have them as sexual persons, as men and women. This fact dictates, in large part, the direction and quality of every subsequent relationship.

In view of the explosion of materials on these subjects for common consumption as well as for sex education courses, the question might be asked, why another book? The answer is that this is not a sex or marriage manual — it is rather an honest search to help young people establish healthy guidelines upon which to build meaning for themselves in love, sex, and marriage. Directed to senior high school students, the book assumes a highly motivated reader with a degree of emotional and intellectual maturity. As such qualifications cannot be lightly presumed of the majority of any group of students, the teacher's guidance of group discussion is essential for giving clarification and proper emphasis to the material. To this end the teacher will find resources in the teaching guide prepared for the course.

The present revision was undertaken because of the changing attitudes that have taken place since 1970 and because some material seemed no longer relevant to youth today. The main points of revision were: first, a clarification of the position of the Church on certain moral issues, and, second, an improved balance in male-female orientation. I expect these changes to make the book more helpful to all readers.

The author wishes to express appreciation for the suggestions from interested teachers, parents, diocesan education personnel, and especially for the contributions of Joan Costello, Maureen Guillou, and Mary Scott who helped greatly in this revision.

Hugo L. Hurst, C.F.X.

What Is the Meaning of Love?

1

Love: A Discussion of the Question

There is no area of human communication that has not attempted to define love or convey its meaning to us. Because the expression of love is multidimensional in its effects, it touches the whole person in his or her physical, psychological, and spiritual being. For this reason there are as many definitions as there are people.

Only in actual communication with other persons do men and women find any meaning. Further, the romantic ideal of song and story has long been considered the basis of true love: Desire, union, presence, concern for others, giving and sharing, mutual trust, response to another, responsibility for someone, affirmation of another, willing good to another, openness, total commitment, and self-donation — these are some of the expressions used to convey the idea of human love. Finally, to add to the confusion of what love is, there seem to be many types of love: love of father and mother, love of parents and children, love of boys and girls, love of friends, love of God and man.

What is the meaning of love?

This short consideration raises many questions. Are personal encounter and communication with others really what love is? Or is the romantic ideal of song and story the real love? Is there one identical ingredient, a common denominator in all love which can describe every expression of love? What is love, and how can we tell if we really love someone?

This section will attempt to probe the meaning of love and to search for the answers to these questions. Hopefully, the resultant knowledge will produce an appreciation of the *powerful* role love plays in our lives. After all, we live in relation to others around us. We are dependent on them and they on us. For this reason, we must form some type of personal relationships with those whom we come in contact with. Love can be this relationship, and it can furnish us with the strongest motive for orienting our lives toward generosity.

It is possible we reach out to others in vain because we do not dare to give ourselves in love. A personal experience of life, however, suggests that love for other human beings is not just something we find and experience alongside other pleasures in life. On the contrary, love is a person relating with his or her total being. It seems, therefore, that the secret of life and of the world around us is some kind of love: We must choose whether to love or to perish.

To arrive at an adequate knowledge of what love is all about, it is first necessary to understand the part love plays in basic human relationships and in everyday personal contacts. To do this it is necessary to analyze in some detail the present attitude of our culture toward love and the values that operate in our daily personal relationships. Many of our attitudes, values, and practices are influenced to a high degree by the current cultural pattern. We are the products of our times to a large extent. We must, therefore, come to appreciate the good and bad ways in which culture speaks to every individual.

The first part of this section takes a critical look at what people call love in human life and culture. From the ideas resulting from this discussion and evaluation, we will attempt in the next chapters to define love in general terms and to describe its qualities as they find expression in everyday life. Finally, this definition, together with its qualities and expressions, will be examined in the light of Christ's command to love all men.

2

What Are People's Attitudes Toward Love?

Although we may find it difficult to put our ideas and feelings into words, the fact remains that all of us have some idea of what love is really all about. At one time or other, in some degree no matter how slight, we have loved or been loved. What is it that we thought and felt? How do we describe what happened? In this section we will search out some of our ideas, feelings, and attitudes toward love. This will be difficult because the experience of love is hard to put into words that others will understand.

Some basic questions

All of us put some value on love, and this directly affects our attitudes and actions toward others.

Is love an art, a progressive and continuing thing that grows and develops, something that requires knowledge and effort? Is this the basis of true love?

Or is love a pleasant feeling, a romantic sensation or desire that one happens to fall into by chance if one is lucky, given the right time, moment, and person? In other words, is love a happening?

Or is love something else?

Prevalent cultural attitudes

Every one thinks that love is important. Every one is curious about life and love. Movies, songs, literature, and talk about love, all are evidence that the human desire for love is often insatiable. Through the medium of the communication arts, people are constantly bombarded with customs, values, and practices concerning the meaning of love. The romantic ideal of love is identified with the experience of falling in love. The enchantment and surrender of romantic love and all its sensational and emotional symptoms are proposed as the real core of love. Some translate "I love you" as "I want you" or "I need you," and this is reason enough for love. "You are cleverer than I am, so you can resolve my doubts; you are physically beautiful and desirable, so you can satisfy my passions; you are a virtuous person, so you can teach me goodness." These attitudes and many more current ones indicate that most people think that *there is nothing to be learned about love* — it just happens to an individual by chance. Love is natural to all of us, so why worry about it — let it happen. Is this what love is all about?

Is there nothing to be learned about love?

That many have such an attitude is clear by the current emphasis on the physical and psychological aspects of love. Women and men, both as lover and loved, react to the physical being as well as to the personality of another. If one asks a boy what is the first thing he looks for in a girl, he is most likely to answer, "Her looks." On second thought he may qualify the statement by adding, "A good personality." The girl may center her attraction on the boy's character, personality, tenderness or affection. It is easy to experience the physical attraction of another, as well as infatuation with his character and personality. However, can knowledge of the physical appearance and the personality of another be reason enough for love? What about the inner core of the person, the other as a spiritual being, the source of

What Are People's Attitudes Toward Love? 19

all that he is and can be? Is there something more to be learned about a person and about love than just the physical and psychological aspects?

Many who say there is nothing to be learned about love see the problem as one of *being loved* rather than *of loving*. Being loved to them is interpreted in these terms: "Can I be lovable to others?" Love, in this case, is what one does or what he or she puts on to be considered "in." This formula for acceptance or attraction is every-changing. For men the formula may be sex appeal, popularity, power, success, social status, money, clothes, a car, athletics. For women the formula may be body measurements, good looks, personality, tenderness, clothes, sensitivity, being a good listener, being fun to be with, or having good manners. These change with the times, but the idea of attraction remains the same.

There are any number of things the male and female can put on or acquire that will make them more attractive and desirable, that is, more lovable. The attitudes of having or possessing another express the idea of being loved. If we consider the problem as one of loving, we are talking about one's capacity to love.

"Do I possess the necessary qualities to love, to give myself to another? Can I really love another? What is my basic attitude toward people? Love seems to be an active power that moves out to others rather than something that I put on to attract others. I must also allow love to touch my inner core. Maybe I have reached out to others in vain because I have never dared to be touched myself. I am afraid to love, or to risk my love, or to give myself to someone."

Others who state that there is nothing to be learned about love see the problem entirely in terms of the person or thing to be loved. They say that to love (the *faculty of loving*) is easy, but finding the right person (the *object to be loved*) to love is the real difficulty.

Will I ever find the right person to love, and when I do will I be happy? How can I be sure that I am in love and not infatuated with this person?

When we see the problem as finding the right *object to be*

loved, we tend to take people for granted, using them because of something they can give us or do for us. Our attraction to them is motivated by desire, by advantages for ourselves, or by a physical or psychological need.

The resulting personal satisfaction becomes reason enough for giving or sharing love. In effect, one is treating others as commodities for one's own use and pleasure: as dispensers for paper in school, as bodies to cuddle and make out with on a date, as stepping-stones for acceptance or popularity with the group. It is easy to use cars, good looks, social status, a pleasing personality, brains, athletic ability, and money to enhance one's ego. This list changes with each age of teens as well as with each section of the country. It is not enough that one has these talents; what matters is how one looks at them and what one does with them. In our culture, in which material success and commodity orientation are the outstanding values and freedom in love is the accepted thing, it is not surprising that human love is often considered in terms of the "right object" to be loved.

In this view, there is little respect for persons considered in themselves. We tend to treat others as means only, as things that cannot think and understand. We should know what people are, what they can be, and what they ought to be. If people remain empty of content, they easily fall into the rigidity of customs and the stereotypes favored by society's traditions.

Considering the problem in terms of the *faculty of loving,* we are talking about a power of the human being which moves out to persons rather than to things. To love is to will good to another in the same way one might will good to oneself. In love people see more than the looks and personality of the person. Love penetrates to that which is unique and valuable for itself, to that which makes a person what he or she is. If we really know *how to love,* finding the right person to love is a lesser problem. It is much more difficult to love than to find the right person to love.

One of the problems about learning to love is the confusion between the initial experience of *falling in love* and the permanent state of *being in love*. One of life's exhilarating experiences is falling in love. Two people who were once strangers now feel a oneness with each other never before experienced. Under the power of their emotions, they become responsive to the body and to the touch of the beloved. The experience finds each lover magnetized by someone who really understands and cares, a person who is really fun to be with. A person's inner excitement in response to the beloved's attractiveness leads to dreams and daydreams. Each becomes aroused and predisposed in thought and action to explore, to have, and to possess the object of love.

It is an exciting time for the young because at this time love begins to reveal its splendor. It gives a person someone to talk to openly and honestly, someone who accepts how one feels, someone who returns affection and love.

All of these are new experiences possible in a human relationship. Falling in love time and time again is not uncommon in youth, yet each new experience of love is really growth in love. Such experiences are usually necessary for the full flowering of love in a person. However, the kind of love described here, though necessary, is by its very nature temporary, intensely emotional, often physical, and infatuating in character. It seldom lasts or leads to an enduring marriage because it is stirred only by the other's physical appearance and personality, not by the other's spiritual core. This kind of love is not mature and lasting love. It is only a stage in the growth toward true love, a part of young love and dating.

The state of being in love, on the other hand, has a permanency which must withstand antagonisms, loss of intimacy, selfishness, disappointments, mutual boredom, setbacks, sickness, and loss. The test of true love is time and difficulty. Being in love means moving outwards, passing from the attitude of "I want to be loved" to "I want to love." And once a person has accepted another with all his or her faults and qualities, one is *in* love. This is the stuff on which a marriage is built. Love and dating between teenagers are a kind of training ground for a much fuller life in marriage which is, not one summer together, but fifty summers.

Conclusion

We started this chapter by asking the question: What are our attitudes toward love? In our search we have probably raised more questions than we answered. In any case, we may now be more conscious of the attitudes and values that actually operate in our everyday personal relationships. We can conclude, however, that there is a great difference between thinking of love as an art requiring knowledge and effort and thinking of love as a chance happening. Yet it is possible that at this stage of our lives, we have experienced love more as a happening than as an art. It is now necessary to probe deeper into the meaning of love.

The *basic problem* of love is made up of current attitudes, practices, and values that operate in our culture and in our lives. We must learn continually from the experiences of life and love so that we can grow to a more mature understanding of what love contributes to life — its pleasure, happiness, peace, and fulfillment. Each of the attitudes discussed so far seems to limit love. Can our expectations of what love is ever be realized in our day-to-day living? What kind of love brings fulfillment to a person?

The *basic premise* adopted in this chapter is that love is an art that requires knowledge and effort. It is not just a chance happening between two people. Therefore, there is something to be learned about love.

3

Love Considered as Union

Anyone who has ever loved someone has had the experience of union. In some way or other, the lover was one with the beloved. The two-in-one-flesh union in marriage conveys this truth. What this union is and how it is constituted is difficult to explain, but the fact remains that love is a kind of fusion. The lover participates in the loved one's thoughts, emotions, actions, values, joys, sufferings, successes, failures, strengths, and weaknesses. The stronger the love, the deeper the fusion. When a person loves, she or he wants to act for the other, to further the fusion in all the familiar aspects of life, and to find new things and ways to share. This is implied by the idea of union.

The basic problem of human life, as Erich Fromm sees it in his book, *The Art of Loving,* is to overcome separation and loneliness. The only adequate solution for that problem, he says, is the union which is love. The question remains: Can every type of union be called love? What really constitutes this union in love? This part of Section One will deal with five ways in which man can and does seek union. From this discussion we should come up with enough ideas to formulate an adequate definition of love.

The paradox and mystery of union

The problem of love is always linked to the problem of life and death — the history and meaning of humanity. It is obvious that one's ideas of love will depend in great part on one's ideas of humankind. Today, as in past ages, man tries to define the human being. Gabriel Marcel, the existentialist philosopher, in his book *Man Against Society,* focuses his attention on what he calls "mass Man," man who has been dehumanized in a society which tends to reduce persons to the functions they perform.

In such a society the individual has no distinctive worth or value and cannot claim to be unique and irreplaceable. The worst danger in this, as Marcel sees it, is that people may come to accept this abstract view of the human being as final. More to the point, Marcel says, "The West has created a society which resembles a machine. It forces men to live in the heart of this society and to adapt themselves to the laws of the machine." Another existentialist, Jean-Paul Sartre, holds a no less critical view of humanity when he says, "Hell is the other person."

In the face of such pessimism it is no wonder that we find it difficult to arrive at an adequate definition of life and of love. We are fighting an uphill battle against the culture's view of the value and dignity of contemporary man. Do we really think that we are worth something all by ourselves? That the fight is on is a fact — people have been dropping out of modern society to find another and simpler way of life. The hippies, the war activists, the black and brown and red power advocates, the new left and the many angry young men and women in the country have done us a service by fighting the establishment and by putting the problems of American culture and modern society into perspective for us. We need not become one of society's protesters, but we can begin to think and to act positively, freely, and independently about life, love, and humanity.

The temporary quality of human life is an important factor in its meaningfulness. The meaning of human existence is based upon its irreversible quality: "You go this way only once." Further, uniqueness and singularity are also essential characteristics of the meaningfulness of human existence because the life of human beings is essentially concrete and subjective.

Therefore, every person, no matter of what status, is summoned to bring alive his or her unique and singular possibilities. Each person has unique opportunities every day to realize this potential, and no one is justified in insisting upon personal inadequacies or demeaning those potentialities.

Though it is not up to a person always to question life, he will in fact always be questioned by life. Each person must respond and answer *to* life by answering *for* his or her own life. The person with no meaning in life is left without moral reserves with which to gain personal peace.

Let us now consider another view of the human being. Everyone is born a person in and for oneself, completely separated from realities outside himself, actually isolated and distinct from the reality of others. As a separated individual a person is, in a sense, a world unto himself, and this one will remain forever. No one will ever be absorbed into any other being, not even into God. Yet this awareness of oneself as a separate and distinct entity, of one's short span of life, of the past and of possibilities for the future, of separateness and aloneness, of seeming helplessness before the forces of nature, culture, and society — all these things make a separate existence from others an almost unbearable prison. A person would probably become insane if he or she could not become liberated by reaching outside and *uniting* in some way or other, with people and the world outside.

Human nature and the human condition demand that a person have contact with others or else die as a human being. Psychologists have shown that babies from birth need physical handling and care to survive. If left on their own too much, they pick up all kinds of diseases and physical ailments. Thus really to live means to seek union with other beings. People possess the equipment for union: Intellectual powers enable one to know reality as truth — for self and others; appetitive powers enable him to desire as well as to seek reality as good — for self and others; locomotive powers enable him to possess reality — for self and others. Thus love can be considered as a basic attitude toward being and life, a union of those separated by the act of existence.

Further, the universe is an ever-changing, dynamic unity, teeming with matter and life. Matter and life reach the highest development in the human being because of his resemblance to the Creator. And because of this unique position in the universe, people have been charged with conveying to God the response which the universe must give concerning existence, fulfillment, and love. This response to God is not automatic, compulsory, instinctive; it is not the blind obedience of an impersonal universe. It is free — a dialogue between two free beings, God and man. This is the possibility, value, dignity, and grandeur of humanity. If God had produced a world in which physical and moral evil were impossible, people would not have the freedom of choice which is pre-supposed in the experience of re-uniting love.

Yet for a person to seek union through love with others is both a paradox and a mystery: born an individual, alone but free, trying to know and find oneself as a person, one also seeks union in dependence on others for fullness of life. This double tendency is the source of tension and anxiety. However, it is both the triumph and the fulfillment of love that it is able to re-unite the most radically separated beings — human beings. A person's basic problem is discovering what kind of union will overcome the separateness and aloneness that is so much a part of life. An individual certainly will achieve some type of union, but not necessarily love. The great danger is that one may achieve some kind of union, healthful or otherwise, without ever experiencing the depth and peace of love. Whether one reaches this stage depends upon which view of humanity he decides to accept. The approaches to union described here may help us in our search for meaning in love, sex, and marriage.

Ways people have attempted to achieve union

Union with another opens up all sorts of possibilities for a human being — fidelity, faith in another, hope, and especially love. There is not only the possibility of realization but realization itself. In union with another, what really matters is that each partner recognizes or discovers himself or herself in the other without losing in the process any part of what is his or her inner being. A person, a free being, can shut off other people and treat them as objects. Yet two human beings can also open themselves to each other in a free, inner movement of love, by which they break through their narrow individuality and thus become themselves.

Throughout history, people have tried to overcome aloneness, to achieve union or identification with other people. In fact, it is the essence of the lot of human beings that they are always sharing a situation with others, the here and now. While all these situations, whatever they may be — worship, military conquest, indulgence in pleasure or luxury, ascetic renunciation, obsessional work — satisfy some basic human need, not all of these are healthful or completely satisfying with regard to human existence and human possibilities.

We will now consider some obvious ways people have attempted to achieve union to relieve the tension and anxiety caused by separateness and aloneness. What we have to determine is if these ways are part of love. In general we will choose the ways discussed by Erich Fromm in his book, *The Art of Loving*. We will not necessarily take either his point of view or his direction. Further, it is not to be implied that the ways described here exhaust the ways in which to achieve union. These were chosen because they seem to be the most common ways.

The first way people attempt to achieve union with others is *orgiastic union*. This is a type of fusion that contemporary society has adopted from our primitive ancestors. For primitive peoples this type of union resulted from the ritualistic practices of individuals trying to achieve identification with the group or community. Principally found in puberty rites, these *orgies* were highly sexual in nature and were normally induced by drugs and alcohol. They were intensely emotional and physical experiences involving the whole person — body, mind, and spirit. Because of their intensity, these rites were usually transitory and periodic, occurring only when tension and anxiety brought about a need to fuse with the group.

These practices have a counterpart in contemporary society. The young even use the term "orgy." One can easily apply the description, characteristics, and name of these primitive orgies to some of the wild parties and "happenings" found in American life. This is true of adult as well as teenager gatherings. The emphasis is on fun, pleasure, and anything sensational. Heavy drinking and alcoholism, pill popping and drug addiction, sex deviation, wild driving, the brutality of some sports, the violence on and off our streets, and the rise in suicide so prevalent in modern life are often no more than desperate attempts, *orgiastic* in character, to escape the anxieties, pressures, and tensions of a lonely existence and of the monotony of life.

A five-day week of monotonous rushing around and two days of fun are usual. The "thank God it's Friday" attitude is a symptom of the problem. As one of the pop hits, talking about this Monday to Friday routine, puts it, "and then we have the weekend to paint the town." On weekends and holidays, when the frantic pace of work or school subsides, all the aimlessness, meaninglessness, and emptiness of life rises up before people once more. Trying to escape this feeling, some find satisfaction in clubs or bars. The music is loud and boisterous, and eliminates the need of talking. People don't have to make an effort at conversation. There is no necessity to think or really communicate; small talk will do the trick. Still others find refuge in sports or books or food, but the cause and effects are the same. And the complaint is ever the same — there is nothing to do.

All these practices result in an ever increasing aloneness because these acts and their effects on people tend to widen rather than bridge the gap between them. Maybe people have forgotten how to relax with and relate to others naturally without the aid of artificial means. Many Americans don't seem to know how to use their leisure, tending to become a nation of spectators who always expect to be entertained. Somehow initiative and creativity must be restored to our lives, especially in the use of leisure. Orgiastic practices do not solve the problem of union because they are artificial, temporary, and too physical to bring about true union.

The form of union with reality chosen by most people is *union by conformity* in which a person conforms to the customs, practices, value systems, and beliefs of the group. It is a union in which the individual disappears to a large extent to be replaced by the social group which determines the acceptable standards and values. This is conformity in essentials. It is not to be confused with conformity in the accidental aspects of life which really don't affect the core of the person.

Our discussion here is concerned with essential conformity, though it may not be named as such. Essential conformity has a certain permanence about it because it is calm, secure, and dictated by routine. Conformity makes so few demands on people as persons, and its results are desirable: status, recognition, and security. What really counts is "I belong." The rationale behind conformity is the belief that if a person wants to be considered "in," he must accept what the group, society, or culture says is important.

There are many unwanted effects involved in allowing ourselves to live a life of conformity. The danger is an uneasy sense of emptiness, of anonymity: a person moves with the forces that sweep him along in the current crowd. It is as if parents, teachers, and society have life all planned for young people, and there is no room for personal choices. Society says a person must go to college to get a good job so that he or she can marry well and have a comfortable life in a split-level house in the suburbs and live happily ever after.

Americans are just beginning to wake up to the price they are paying for such conformity — and the psychiatrist is getting most of what they are paying. A man who has rejected conformity is Fletcher Waller, who a few years ago was working fourteen hours a day as vice-president of Bell and Howell. He loved sailing, but he could never get his boat out because he didn't have the time. So at 52 he quit his job and started his own business, renting boats and teaching boating to over-worked executives. Waller's income was considerably reduced, but he laughed at *Who's Who* for dropping him from their list of notables. Describing the effect of the change on his marriage, he says, "Why, we fell in love."

This does not happen to everyone, but it is just one example of a growing number of Americans who are fighting the forces of conformity and learning how to live. In February 1967 *Newsweek* magazine carried this editorial, "Advice to a bored young man: Died age 20; buried age 60. The sad epitaph of too many Americans. Mummification sets in on too many young men and women at the age when they should be ripping the world wide open . . . Go do something about it."

If life is to be saved from the boredom of conformity, relieved only by disasters and extraordinary events, means must be found for restoring individual initiative, for things that really matter. As the philosopher Schopenhauer puts it, "Human life dangles between trouble and boredom." Uncertainty and fear may plague the way for those who want to become unique persons, but the decision to open a new door in life is far better than accepting a life of conformity dictated only by society. Life is not just anything; it is really the opportunity for something that an individual thinks is important.

The incidence of alcoholism, drug addiction, compulsive sexuality, and suicide are just symptoms, psychologists tell us, of the failure of herd conformity to pacify the anxiety of separateness and aloneness. People need bigger kicks just to keep out of the doldrums of despair. Some try to take their minds off their problems by narcotizing their feelings. The essence of intoxication is a turning away from the objective world and turning toward the subjective world of one's own making. This solves nothing because it does not confront the cause of the problem.

In concrete and practical terms, conformity has come to mean the *elimination of differences*. For example, a person could eliminate differences through *uniformity* in dress, customs, ideas, values, and mores which are dictated by the group or society. While no man is an island, few Americans are willing to stand up and be counted. It is a paradox, however, that in the freest society in the world, people are willing to conform much more than they really have to. So much conformity and uniformity, sociologists tell us, is the result of mass man, the product of our highly technological, industrialized, and urban society, one in which a person must not make too many waves.

In the face of big-government, big-labor, big-city, big-everything, Americans are forced to ask certain questions: How does a human being make his or her life count for something? How does an individual maintain an identity and achieve fulfillment? How can a person confront the complexities of mass society so that the freedom, independence, initiative, and creativity of the individual survive?

The elimination of differences is also found in the idea of *equality*. Erich Fromm points up the difficulty: "Equality has meant, in a religious context, that we are all God's children, that we are all one. It meant also that the very differences between individuals must be respected; that while it is true we are all one, it is also true that each of us is a unique entity, is a cosmos by itself." Is this what is understood by equality today? Theoretically perhaps, but not in the practical experiences of life. American society seems to put a higher value on *sameness* than on *oneness*. For example, men and women are equal in that they are not really different, except physically. The natural polarity of the sexes (men and women being physically and psychologically complementary, like the poles in a magnet) is said to be disappearing, and with it the natural source of erotic attraction and love. Some psychologists even go so far as to say the incidence of sexual deviation, frigidity in women, and impotence in men, is the result of the lack of proper sex identity. In some segments of American life the male differs little from the female in looks, actions, or dress. Are men and women becoming the same rather than equals? Many men and women are fighting this tendency to *sameness*. Women's liberation, while working for equality, has also stressed woman's femininity.

If equality is to be rescued from the monotony of *sameness* and restored to its original idea of *oneness,* every person must first come to value herself or himself as unique. Difference is the spice of life that fosters knowledge and real communication. Blacks have found this out and are attempting to break the narrow categories and stereotypes into which white society has tended to classify them. Every man and woman must be conscious of a positive self worth, apprehend oneself in one's own uniqueness if one is ever to be present to and cherish the self in union with another. A person who is never really conscious of uniqueness and individuality, who is really unable to say, "I really am my own person," is equally incapable either of loving oneself or others. Can true union and love be possible when we understand equality as sameness and not as uniqueness?

Finally, the elimination of differences can come about by *routine in work and play.* In the past few years, much has been written about the work and leisure habits of Americans. An examination of contemporary life seems to indicate that the whole of man's life — his work, play, pleasure, and leisure — is becoming mechanized and packaged. The American worker is a nine-to-fiver, a part of a large labor force, who is supposed to perform certain tasks prescribed by the organization. Technology and the economy are accused of feeding on the souls and psyches of men and women for sources of energy, emasculating laborer and manager alike, and turning them into gray-faced status-seeking consumers. Everyone and everything is viewed as a commodity. Hard work has come to mean efficiency, and success has become bigness. If you really want to crush and punish a person completely, says philosopher-mathematician Bertrand Russell, just make his work absolutely pointless and absurd. For housewives the monotony of preparing perhaps a thousand meals a year can be frustrating, and many housewives are beginning to voice their discontent with a job on which society does not place enough value.

All these pressures and distorted values can lead to emptiness, monotony, and blandness of life — *you move with the forces that aim you.* If society can retail emotions and package love, pleasure, and recreation, no wonder that people have a sense of aloneness and alienation. People seem to live in a carefree, love-free, and painfree society — that is, if they take the right pills. Hedonism, pleasure for pleasure's sake, has found a friend in contemporary men and women. Those who have no goal in life are running the course of life at the highest possible speed so that they will not notice the aimlessness of it. They are trying to run away from themselves. Initiative is so stifled that no one really rises to the top because there is no room there to be different, creative, and free. Vast numbers of people are hard at work all week, and on Saturday and Sunday are overwhelmed by the emptiness and lack of content in their lives which two days of idleness bring into consciousness.

The dignity of the human being forbids his being used as a means, becoming a mere instrument of the labor or managerial process, being degraded to a means of production. The person who is entirely devoted to earning money, who is busy earning the means for living, is in a position to forget life itself. In fact, a person can become so orientated to the future that life will pass him by. He forgets that only today is given to him and he should live it to the fullest. Most important for human life are its quality and richness of content, not work itself.

Even American Christianity has taken on certain aspects of conformity: Uniformity, sameness, and routine. Aldous Huxley has described it as "Christianity without tears": no real challenge, no real temptations, no big falls or weaknesses, pleasant and accommodating vices, easy to manage virtues. In his book, *Brave New World,* Huxley speaks of the homogenized man, all milk and cream where nothing rises to the top. The type of conformity Huxley speaks of is pernicious because it is not imposed from without by force or pressure but grows from within, subconsciously and unnoticed.

This type of conformity can be contrasted with that in George Orwell's *1984,* where conformity is imposed from without. Conformity from within or from without is a far cry from the challenge that Christ gave to all men and women to love God totally and to love others in the measure they love themselves.

So much of what has been said so far about conformity reflects the attitudes of many modern philosophers, principally existentialists, who conclude that life is either absurd or is full of paradoxes and ambiguities. Gabriel Marcel in his book, *Man Against Society,* concludes that if people assume a pessimistic attitude toward life and love, what is lost is themselves — their humanity, their personal concern for others. Next to physical security and psychological stability, a person's highest need is for creativity, initiative, and self-fulfillment. Imagine getting up in the morning, looking at yourself in the mirror, and saying to yourself, "The most important thing I can do today is place four bolts in the right rear end of a car." American society has been accused of failing to ask for or expect any depth of commitment from the individual, and because of its demands for conformity it even discourages such commitment. The question remains: Can conformity produce a true union with others, and can this union be called love?

Another way in which man attempts to achieve union is what Erich Fromm calls *union by creative activity.* Experience tells us that some people unite themselves, as it were, with the material or objects they work with. For example, they say that the artist and his art become one. Here the unity is with an object, not a person. Experience further tells us that, for some, this type of union can take on compulsive and obsessive characteristics. But the artist is not alone in this. Many people at times try to escape from the frightening vastness of life by taking refuge in work. The real emptiness of life comes upon them full force on weekends and vacations. There is nothing to fill the inner void because the person is wholly wrapped up in his work.

Why do people become obsessed with their work — a man with his job, a woman with her career, a student with his studies, an athlete with his sports, a mechanic with his car? Why do people get so involved? The paradox is that while the object (work, studies) can't hurt a person, neither can it really satisfy. Things are not people; things can't and don't fight back while people are human and independent, often hard to know and definitely hard to manage. Yet only people can respond to people, appreciate give and share, participate in one another's lives. Thus a person must come to love more than the qualities of another; he must come to love the person who has the qualities. This means more than loving him or her as just things.

While there is a union of a sort between a person and the object of his work or creative activity, it is impossible that such a union could reach the depths of fusion that can be reached by two persons who love each other. We must continue our search for a kind of union worthy of human love.

Erich Fromm coined the title for the next kind of union which we will discuss — *psychic symbiotic union*. This type of union is based on mutual needs. In the case of male-female relationships, if either person reduces his need and dependence to an immature level, the couple will together develop needs at this abnormal or immature psychological level. This generally results in what psychologists call masochism and sadism. Unfortunately, the man in the street reserves these terms for extreme cases where people show their need in bizarre ways. However, these terms can be applied to any relationship where domination or dependence is present to any degree. If one partner of a personal relationship is used by the other or if both are unhealthfully interdependent on each other, something which seemed to be friendship and love is in reality compulsion and obsession.

Passive symbiotic union is usually called *masochism*. The masochistic person escapes from the feeling of aloneness, says Fromm, by making himself or herself part of another person who guides and protects. This dependence may be great or small according to the psychic need. The person to some degree renounces independence, integrity, and decisions in favor of the person on whom she or he is dependent. A masochist will usually tell every secret to the other, turn the other cheek when pain is inflicted, satisfy the other's every whim even when rejected.

Sexually, the masochist derives erotic pleasure from being humiliated, hurt, or even degraded sexually. Usually if feminine sexuality is weakened in any way, it is transferred into masochism or possessiveness by men. On the other hand, poor male sexual identity can result in hen-pecked husbands. In each case, these people are making demands on each other.

Active symbiotic union is called *sadism*. The sadistic person, according to Fromm, wants to escape from the feeling of aloneness by making another a part of himself by commanding, exploiting, hurting, or humiliating the other person. His obsession is to dominate the other and his pleasure is to inflict pain, either mental or physical. When the paralysis of masculinity or feminity becomes extreme in a man or woman, sadism becomes the main perverted substitute for it. A man needs to prove his virility; a woman needs to be loved and wanted. Sexually, the sadist derives his erotic pleasure from inflicting physical or mental pain on his partner or by humiliating the person by perverted acts of sex. Psychologists tell us that much of the psychology of the whore is directed to her desire to degrade men.

In the case of either masochism or sadism there is a union without integrity. In a mature union, the integrity, individuality, and uniqueness of both persons are preserved. *Symbiotic* union is submission to or domination of the other; however, such dependence or domination cannot be classified as true union because of its compulsive and abnormal character. Though some may want to call this relationship a kind of love because it satisfies mutual needs, it seems at best to be an immature and unsatisfactory union.

At this point we need to distinguish masochistic and sadistic tendencies from leadership qualities. The question here is how people act when put in positions of authority over others, how they treat people under them. The leader must work for the common good of the followers; in a sense the leader is a reflection of the common will. A sadist tends to inflate himself and his worth by being ruthless with those who follow him or her, usually demanding blind obedience. On the other side of the coin, how do people act under the leadership of another? Do they think for themselves, or do they act like lambs being led to slaughter?

Finally, we will discuss what is probably one of the easiest and most natural forms of union to achieve —*physical and psychic union* between two persons. Besides the universal human desire for union, there exists between men and women a more specific, biological desire as well as a psychic desire for love and union. The natural physical and psychic polarization of the male and female leads a person to bridge the gap by union with another in a specific way — sexual intercourse. In this sexual union, there may or may not be love. If there is love, it expresses itself in the psychic aspects of the union as well. This natural male-female polarity is the fundamental basis for interpersonal creativity and union, physical as well as psychic. The sexual function in the person is the power to carry the psychic love and physical union between two persons to the point of creating new life. The sex instinct, therefore, is a distinct impulse to creative love in marriage as finally expressed in procreation.

In the experience of love, men and women react differently to the physical, psychic, and spiritual aspects of the human person. Thus the bodily appearance of the opposite sex is sexually arousing, and this arousal sets off the sex drive. As a consequence, the person is desirous of union with a sex partner. However, sexual desire is only one manifestation of the need for love and union.

While sexual attraction is certainly motivated by the need to remove sexual tension, it is mainly the need for union with the other sexual pole that is the principal source of desire and subsequent satisfaction. In fact, erotic attraction is by no means embodied solely in physical characteristics. The masculine-feminine character and personality traits also have great appeal and attraction to the opposite sex. A lover's emotionality is stirred by the particular psyche of the other, by the particular character traits of the person, his or her temperament and dispositions. These points will be discussed more fully later in the section on human sex and sexuality.

Because the sexes are complementary and therefore really

different (not just physically), they always remain somewhat of a mystery to one another. In fact, the love which joins them actually thrives upon this reciprocal mysteriousness. Masculinity has traditionally contained such qualities as penetration, guidance, activity, discipline, adventurousness, aggressiveness, abstraction, decision, firmness. Femininity has been presumed to include receptiveness, protection, realism, endurance, motherliness, tenderness, intuition, dependence, emotionality, gentleness. In point of fact, both men and women have the potential for many of these descriptive traits on both lists.

Many in the woman's liberation movement would disagree strongly with these traditional descriptions of maleness-femaleness. Further, psychologists tell us that if character traits are weakened because emotionally one has remained a child, a person will try to compensate for this lack by extreme emphasis on either the male or female role in sex. For example, the Don Juan and the Sex Pot need to prove sexual prowess because they are unsure of their sex identities or roles in sex. Homosexuality and lesbianism are other examples of such weakened sex identities and represent a failure to achieve polarized union. The cause of both problems is psychological as we understand them today.

It is obvious from what has been said that *physical and psychic union* is both healthful and good. The question that immediately comes to mind is: Does physical and psychic union constitute love? It would seem so because desire is such a natural part of every love relationship and experience. Upon further analysis, our experience also tells us that physical and psychic states are not permanent. Sexual excitement is only temporary; the sex drive vanishes after gratification. And infatuation, the result of psychic attraction, is seldom of long duration. It is true that some people get hung up on either the physical or psychic aspects of a person. All they talk about is their sexual prowess or how much fun they have making out or about the personal characteristics of their latest love. Viktor Frankl in his book, *The Doctor and the Soul,* refers to the physical and psychic aspects of the personality as the outer dress of the inner core of the person which he calls the spiritual being. Experience indicates that love is something permanent and enduring which reaches beyond the physical and psychic aspects of a person as we have described them. Love is concerned with the person — the spiritual being — as unique, irreplaceable, and incomparable. Love does not care as much about particular physical or personality characteristics as it does about what the person is in his or her uniqueness. As a unique person, he or she is irreplaceable. Therefore, love seems to be much more than anything that we have discussed up to this point. The question remains: What really constitutes the essence of love? Or is love as varied as man's experience and hence cannot be defined?

Conclusion

Up to this point in our presentation, we have been rather tough in our evaluation of American culture in its attitude and practice toward life and love. Some may object that the viewpoint taken here has been too one-sided and negative, that no attempt was made to present the positive aspects and accomplishments of our culture. In a way this criticism is justified. There are several reasons, however, for taking the approach that we did. Americans constantly are bombarded by the communications media with rationales for accepting the romantic ideal for love, sex, and marriage. This ideal is sold as a commodity and is not the stuff that life is made of. By putting in bold perspective the problems that our culture faces concerning a meaningful idea of love, we are better able to search out the ideas about love and the value put on them. In the process, we became more conscious and critical of the soft-sell reasoning that is so often encountered.

It would also seem that more has been said about what love is not than about what it is. This approach may seem more confusing than enlightening. We have just considered five ways in which man attempts to overcome his separateness and achieve union with others: orgiastic union, union by conformity, union by creative activity, psychic symbiotic union, and physical and psychic union. The point is that all these ways, to some degree, *fulfill a need* for a person, but simple satisfaction of a need is not necessarily love. Since these ways do not necessarily open up a person to the transcendent possibilities that love offers us as human beings, they must be considered a failure as love — though some of them may well be a part of love's expression. The critical analysis we used in evaluating the ways a person can and does reach out for union with another opened up many ideas that will help us to formulate a working definition of love.

However we define love, we must now say that love is a union, but it is a union that preserves one's independence, individuality, and uniqueness. The more one strives to be an individual, the more one advances toward perfect integrity and authenticity. Only then is one able to reach out to others in a union we can call love.

The key to the problem of union seems to be that a person cannot love and achieve true union with another human being unless one is mature. To love another for what he or she is essentially, one must first be able to stand alone as a mature person. Anything less must be considered immature love. True love cannot be based on need or dependence whether it be physical, psychological, economic, cultural, sociological, sexual, ethical, or emotional. If a person is moved to union with another to satisfy a need, that person cannot love the other for himself or herself alone but only for something he or she can give.

The problem young men and women face is knowing when they are attracted to another for selfish reasons and knowing when they are loving the other because that person is lovable. A young person need not be fully mature, however, to "fall" into what becomes a true love. What is needed is enough maturity to forget oneself in the love relationship. When both lovers can do this, each one matures and grows, for love promotes maturity and strength in the person. And if the love relationship keeps a basically unselfish outlook, the love will grow even more mature as the years go by. Like flowers growing from a seed, mature love opens up many beautiful dimensions in the lovers' lives. From these considerations, we conclude that love requires both effort and knowledge, that it is an art, that there is indeed something to be learned about love.

4

A Definition and Description of Love

We have been considering various aspects of love and union. In the process we have touched upon many ideas that can now be more fully considered to help us understand what is meant by love. In a sense, the approach may have appeared critical and negative; it did force us, however, to examine our own feelings and convictions. What follows is a discussion of the qualities that are part of every love relationship. Finally, we will take a look at ways in which love expresses itself in our lives. This should widen the possibilities for meaning in love.

Jean Mouroux in his book, *The Meaning of Man,* speaking about the paradoxes of love, says, "love is passivity and activity, union and movement, affectivity and liberty, spirit and flesh, desire and gift." But what does this definition mean? The inadequacy of our language and ideas make it extremely difficult to express the highest and deepest experiences of love. Whatever love is in its true meaning, most people think of it as a mysterious and deeply moving force. The literature, music, and art of all times and cultures testify to this natural conviction. There is certainly value to be put on the spontaneous testimony of those who have experienced love, especially those who are generally considered to have loved most intensely and maturely. We must now ask ourselves: Is there some common aspect in our love experiences which will lead us to a general concept of love? Is there one element which is constant in all love?

A working definition of love

To answer these questions, let us first look at some definitions that men through the ages have proposed. It is easy to confuse love with its consequences, conditions, and expressions. Love has been variously defined as desire (Plato, Freud, Tillich), joy (Spinoza), benevolence (Aristotle, Aquinas), response (Buber, Toner), union (Fromm), and affirmation (Ortega y Gasset, Toner). Other descriptions that have been proposed are: presence, adherence, concern and care for someone, relating positively to another, taking responsibility for someone, and giving of self. All of these seem to touch upon a real experience of love. Before we try to organize them into a working definition of love, however, let us first try to analyze briefly some of these basic ideas. In this analysis we will generally follow Jules Toner's outline as contained in his book, *The Experience of Love*.

Love can be qualified by one of two relationships that the lover has with the object of his love, whether present or absent. These are either *desire* or *joy*. *Love as desire* is one of the most common experiences of man. It is a tendency (desire, urge, movement) of the lover to possess the object of his love. The source of the desire may be the physical, psychic, or spiritual qualities of the beloved. When the lover takes possession of the beloved in love, desire is satisfied, and it would seem that love ends. If we define love simply as desire, we rob love of its depth and richness, for love is more than just desire for another. On the other hand, *love as joy* is the delight or rejoicing in the loved one, the happiness and peace in the presence of the other, a sort of affirmation of a person's value as a person. Here joy results from possession and resting in the object of love. Again we must ask: But what happens to love once one possesses the object of love? What keeps it going?

We are probably getting close to actual experience when we define *love as response* to the total reality of the beloved. A lover responds first to the beloved's actuality, to the fact that he or she "is"; and secondly, a lover responds to the beloved's lovable qualities and actions insofar as these are true expressions of one's personal being — "what" he or she is. Thus in loving, one responds not merely to the qualities of a person but also to the person who has the qualities. This love response releases a new energy in the person.

As a consequence of this energy or power of love, the lover not only breaks the narrowing confines of one's self but also is made more aware of the world and of others. In particular, the lover is able to experience the lives of those whom his love touches and in some way the lover's life and love become theirs. Certainly, the idea of response suggests some of the depths of love as it is experienced.

Anyone who has loved another has had the experience of *love as union*. The idea of union is basic to any definition of love because in some way or other the person who has loved has "lived certainty" that she or he is in some way one with the object of his love. The lover is the loved. Now, love is an active power in human beings, a power which breaks through the walls that separate a person from others, uniting them with one another and thus overcoming their separateness and aloneness. Yet, in the very act of union, love helps a person to be oneself, to retain one's individuality and uniqueness. As love deepens, each grows more sensitive to the other.

What lovers seek in this union is a special way of being *present* to each other, of being one in heart and mind with the other while still respecting the other's individuality. Lovers want to be totally present to each other, but healthy unselfish love allows both persons to grow stronger as unique individuals as well.

This special way that lovers are present to each other comes from the joyous private knowledge that each has given himself or herself to the other, and each has been accepted in return. Instantaneously the lovers know "He's mine" or "She belongs to me", and a sense of identification results. "We will share our lives, everything we have," the lovers think to themselves or tell each other. But happiness flowing from this early giving and sharing of the lovers pales by comparison to the depth of feelings of peace and joy which come to married couples who try to work out day by day what this "gift" really means. The word "work" here is crucial, because problems, choices, health, boredom, and even success can create new situations for a couple requiring decisions and daily adjustments from both. The couple doesn't know what's ahead. Strength will be there in the union if husband and wife have a strong *trust* in each other.

Trust, a crucial factor to giving, to union, to love as saying "yes" to one another, is the magic catalyst that allows the couple to grow and become new people together. Without *trust* that says simply, "I believe you" and "I believe *in* you," the words and physical expression of love become sham, and the hopes of love wither.

Finally, love as it's lived demonstrates that *love affirms* or says "yes" to another. The lover says "Yes" to who and what the other person is. This has to be just as total an acceptance as the lover has for himself or herself as a person. The degree to which a young woman, for example, can affirm her husband as a person in his own right depends on how much she has first been able to accept herself as a lovable person. It's like the childhood game of "Pass it on": love and acceptance can't be given away until it's first been received and experienced. The toddler who has never learned that he is good will have difficulty accepting himself as an adult. The young adult who has a good self-concept and who is unselfish has freedom to be able to say "yes" to the loved one, confirming and affirming him or her as a unique person.

A loved one who is affirmed this way is loved for unique qualities, not as a reflection of the lover, or as some kind of extension of the lover's personality. The high school athlete "in love" with the girl whose whole personality is focused on looking good for him and on following his particular sport is really loving an extension of himself. All love has some element of this, but true love cannot be built on this alone.

Because so much of unselfish love depends on an individual's ability to focus on someone rather than on his or her own needs, we can begin to understand how important it is for young men and women to have formed good self-concepts in childhood. Self-concepts are always present affecting each couple's capacity to affirm each other. Yet strangely enough, a simple and trusting love relationship can build new strong self-concepts in a loved one. For some, like the Marilyn Monroes of this world, a healthy secure love doesn't seem possible; yet for the majority it is possible, in varying degrees, if they so choose.

We are now in a position to put these thoughts together into a working definition of love which will include the ideas of response, union, presence, trust and affirmation: *Love is a unifying response between two people who care for and have said "yes" to each other's total being. It presumes mutual acceptance of each other, freedom and trust, and it seeks the fulfillment and happiness of each other as a common goal.*

Elements in every experience of love

We can now look for certain common elements of true love in every act of human love. While all elements in the above definition may be necessary for a total experience of deep love, they won't be found in every example of true love simply because people have different capacities to love. However, some elements seem to be necessary if love is to exist at all. Among all the possible dimensions of love, we have chosen two which are present in every aspect of love: *love as desire* and *direct love*.

Love as desire looks to the external, observable qualities in a person and hence to what is relative and particular, not unique. The person is attracted to another by the qualities one sees in him or her as a person. As desire, love is a drive toward possession of someone or something outside oneself that will fulfill a lack in oneself, as well as complete the self as a person. Because of this desire, a person looks out to the world, people and things, and seeks to appropriate what he or she needs for perfection and completion as a person.

What is the source of attraction for another person? This is not easy to determine. However, experience suggests that one is attracted to people who have something one likes and lacks. On the other hand, psychologists tell us that a person usually dislikes someone who has the same defects that he has.

Therefore, one loves persons for the good one will get from them or give to them. In the act of love as desire, one possesses the object of love. Love as desire is a tendency to a good not yet possessed, a tendency to a physical and psychological good. No human love as desire occurs without physical manifestations or without the influence of psychic and emotional factors. Let us now consider two expressions of love as desire: *physical* and *psychic* love.

Physical love is the desire of every human being to fulfill himself or herself through physical contact or bodily union with another. It is the basic source of the mutual attraction between male and female. In fact the very physiology of man and woman verifies this desire and need for union, the mutual love of penetration and reception.

Usually the first response people have upon meeting another person is sexual awareness — whether they are male or female — and this fact helps determine the nature of the subsequent relationship. Physical love is usually identified with the desire for sensual self-fulfillment accompanied by pleasure. There is no doubt that love properly speaking is neither this physical union nor bodily contact. These are but signs of the deeper and more lasting union which is true love.

Experience indicates, however, that sexual desire is definitely one manifestation of the need for love and union. The biological aspect of sexuality must not ignore, however, the natural masculine-feminine polarity and the mutual desire to bridge this polarity by some kind of physical contact and union. The bodily appearance of the other person is sexually awakening, and this sets off the sexual desires in a person. If one asks a boy or girl what is the first thing they look for in each other, they will usually start with physical qualities because these are the first things that catch the eye and attract. Watching the girls or boys go by is still a popular sport. An emphasis on friendship puts this sexual aspect in a concrete, healthful perspective.

Though the discussion on physical love has centered principally on the sexual aspects and the male-female relationship, one should not get the impression that all physical love is sexual. Love in friendship also has its physical qualities: Thus one finds in the customs of most peoples physical expressions of love between friends. It may be expressed simply in the evident joy of friendship and companionship, of just being together at work, study, sports, or recreation. The person is present through the medium of sign and gesture. That is why we usually associate gifts and acts of sacrifice with love. These things become the vehicle of a love that exists between persons. The fact remains that love between all persons, male or female, desires to reveal itself to the other in a most human way, in personal radiation expressed in language and gesture, in the glance of the eye and the sound of the voice, in face, figure, and movement.

All love must have some physical way to express itself because a person communicates through his or her body. Customs and culture usually determine the public expressions of physical love. In America, for example, men are embarrassed to express their love to one another by any physical contact except the handshake or other neutral signs; otherwise the tag "homo" is put on them. On the other hand, women are allowed all kinds of outward physical expressions of friendship. A bear hug between men is permitted only after a football game or some other special events or occasions. The growing custom of slapping a guy's hand in meeting may be a sign for the need of men to develop meaningful expressions of friendship.

Sexual desire is only one manifestation of the need for love and union. Sexual attraction between the sexes is only partly motivated by the need for removal of tension. It is mainly the need for union with the other sexual pole. This need for union is more than just physical desire; it is highly psychological in content.

We will now consider the elements of *psychic love,* called by some erotic love. A human being needs others like himself to find psychological equilibrium. The satisfaction of this need is the good one person sees in another, the other's particular psychic characteristics and personality. If you ask boys what they look for in a girl, most will mention physical characteristics first, but then they will qualify this by saying the girl must also have a good personality. Girls react in the same way. They are reflecting the fact that experience tells us we are usually stirred emotionally by the psyche of the other, by the particular character traits, personality, temperament, and dispositions of the one we love. In other words, love goes beyond the mere physical qualities of a person into the personality of the loved one.

Thus true love takes on a creative role in the formation and integration of the human personality and character with the physical qualities. The aim in love is to bring out the ultimate possibilities of the other, to help that person realize her or his potential value as a person. Only in meaningful encounters does one come to realize that the other is a unique ego which finds its physical expression through the psychic characteristics. Therefore, a creative person must develop the psychic expressions of his character and personality by properly integrating the psychic with its physical expressions.

"Why don't people like me? Am I a phony? What do you say and do to help love grow? Do I have a good or bad personality? Why? What can I do about it?"

The answers to these questions will help us to understand the role of the physical and the psychic in the development of personality. *In normal and healthy relationships, the psychic quality of love greatly intensifies the physical quality.* "You're not getting older, you're just getting better," is the way a recent song expresses this psychic quality of love. This trait is noticeably absent in disordered love.

The psychic quality of love finds its most natural expression in infatuation by which the emotions are stirred by the psychic characteristics of the other. The emotional quality of love is the most talked about, most experienced, and probably most misunderstood element of love. It is the love of song and story. Why? There is no love experience without an emotional quality, and this element is often mistaken for love itself. The sexual emotion, in particular, prepares the whole person for action. Love as an emotion involves affection toward the beloved, anticipation at the thought of reunion with the beloved, happiness in the presence of the beloved, passion for and response to the beloved's very being.

Emotional love is not just a passive happening but has the character of an active and spontaneous response to the touch, looks, and person loved. This results in sensitive feelings and a kind of magnetism that stirs the thoughts and predisposes the person to action, to explore and possess the other. In the moment of love, past, present, or future experiences of love are recalled or imagined, resulting in an inner excitement and emotional power that elicits feelings of warmth, passion, affection, happiness, and satisfaction. In the moment of encountering another person, emotional love seeks physical expression. Therefore, it must be properly integrated with physical love and the other psychic expressions of love; otherwise, love as emotion remains a blind power. Because it is an element in all love and is deeply felt by the lover, it can easily be mistaken for love itself. This is particularly true in adolescence. Emotional love must be kept in the whole perspective of love. All the problems of love and human relationships become insolvable if love is basically understood as emotion. Love would be reduced to mere sentimentality.

The second dimension of love is *direct love*. This love is focused on the person; looks to the internal and hidden qualities of the person, to that which is absolute and unique. As such, direct love is a *response* to the other person, an *awareness* of his or her unique value and worth as a human being. This is an *affirmation* of the other's personal being to which the lover is present, and a personal *identification* with the other by which the lover and the other are one. Unlike love as desire, which looks to the person's qualities and attributes, direct love looks to the person's *entire self*, as being in and for itself, and as someone apart from the lover.

One loves another, not as an object to be possessed, but as a subject to be loved in and for herself or himself, for what that person is, just as she or he is. The lover's dream is to render the beloved infinitely lovable, to help the beloved flower in existence, individuality, value, and freedom. Hence in loving the world, in loving society, and in loving fellow human beings, one is on the march toward the love of God.

Direct love is active in that the lover is not just aroused physically by the other nor stirred emotionally, but rather he or she actually is moved to penetrate the unique hidden center of the other. The lover is no longer interested in an alluring physical type or an attractive personality but is concerned with the person as unique, irreplaceable, and incomparable.

Human love in its fullest sense is the experience of a person actually present as a subject (not an object), a self in all the depth of his or her inner mystery.

Two persons in love are for each other a revelation of what it means to be: to exist as a human person who counts for something, to be totally oneself and not be afraid one won't be liked. This is love at the level of what Martin Buber calls an "I and Thou," the mystery of personal communication of two who love each other, two who have experienced and have enjoyed the secret mystery of the individual self.

In such direct love, a person breaks the little circle he forms around himself and discovers a new and separate existence — the other. Having discovered one's own self as a unique value, a person is able to reach out to the other and recognize and appreciate his or her unique value as a person. Therefore, love for the other is based on the value one loves in himself. A friend becomes a new revelation of that value. By recognizing and loving this value in the other, a person cures himself of exclusiveness, poverty, and aloneness. By loving, one opens oneself to the fullness of being, existence, and value in all their variety and mystery as these are exemplified in another person.

Love results in a deeper understanding of the uniqueness of each person.

Such love means coming into direct contact with another as a spiritual being, with the beloved as a unique, free person totally distinct from the lover. As the highest form of love, it breaks through one's small, egocentric world and moves into the center of being of the other, affirming her or him as the other. Of course, this personal center of the other is impossible to describe because it is the inexhaustible source of all that the other is and can be — all his acts, values, attitudes, and qualities as a person.

Viktor Frankl in *The Doctor and the Soul* describes the spiritual core as the carrier of those physical and psychic characteristics to which people are attracted. In other words, the physical and psychic aspects of the personality are like the outer garment which the spiritual core wears. No one can ever really define the person of the other but only the experience of that person. The fact to keep in mind, however, is that this personal center of the other is directly experienced as it is in itself through all the revelations flowing from it. However, as all experience is necessarily limited, people never know a person fully, and hence are continually surprised by every new and lovable quality that he reveals. To the degree that people are mutually open to others, their love will grow in knowledge, depth, fullness, and truthfulness. The consequences of love and the reactions to the person loved are much easier to describe: in the many shades of joy over the other's varying fullness of being which is gradually revealed; in the lover's care and concern for the different needs and desires of the other together with the satisfaction of fulfilling these; in words or in silence, and in the infinite subtleties of time, gesture, look, or smile; in the endless ways of acting, reacting, and enduring; in the unfolding of values and attitudes that operate in another's life; in giving love as well as accepting it — in a word, all the expressions of love that can possibly permeate human life and thus reveal the complex center of the other.

Therefore, the individual grows in love all his life. To be faithful to the dynamism and creativity of his human nature, one should never stop striving to be oneself, to be one's own unique person. In growing, the individual makes others grow and thus enlarges mankind's possibilities. The maxim of Goethe is appropriate: "If we take people as they are, we make them worse. If we treat them as if they were what they ought to be, we help them to become what they are capable of becoming." When through one person a little more love and light, a little more truth, goodness, and beauty comes into the world, then human life gains meaning.

Ways in which love is expressed

We have defined love and explained two dimensions of love found in every love experience. These considerations were an attempt to see love in its fundamental meaning — how it actually works in human beings. We have seen that if we are to grow in life and love and to blossom into maturity, it is necessary to know *what* love is and *how* and *why* it operates in our lives. Consideration of such basic elements may make love seem to be an academic or theoretic reality. In our day-to-day experience, however, love is a many splendored thing, and we will now consider two common ways in which love expresses itself concretely and specifically. While each way will be treated separately for better understanding, true love is a blending of both these expressions.

Before we reflect on the ways that love can be expressed, it is necessary to remember that to express love people must have a certain degree of maturity — that is, they must be able to stand alone as persons.

In practical terms, maturity means that people should possess in some degree: *integrity,* a basic honesty with themselves and others about what and who they are; *individuality,* an ability to stand by themselves as persons with both strengths and weaknesses; *freedom,* a liberation from the disorderly demands of instincts so that they are free to open themselves to all those things and others that can fulfill them at the deepest level; *independence,* a liberation from the pressures of culture, imposed value systems, as well as coercion from family and friends, so they can be what they are and ought to be as unique persons possessing dignity and value.

Let us now consider the two expressions of love. Human experience indicates that all love expresses itself as a *giving* by the lover and an *acceptance* of the love by the beloved. Most people understand giving as a sort of "giving up" or sacrificing something, and accepting as the receiving of a gift or favor. Giving and accepting are among the highest expressions of human presence and aliveness. The presence of the lover in the beloved and of the beloved in the lover involves the notion of self-giving and acceptance. Loving is spoken of as giving self and being loved is spoken of as being accepted.

In giving love to another, one experiences oneself as overflowing, spending, alive. In accepting the love of another, one experiences oneself as becoming alive through another. If a person doesn't possess these qualities, he or she can't give. Most important is the desire to give love to another or accept love from another.

It is the right of every person to demand something from others: even in the most impersonal relationships one must be acknowledged as a person. This is the bare minimum; the maximum is self-sacrifice, my life for another. How much is one willing to give? Most people don't know until they are faced with the question in everyday life. Yet the fact is that people daily have the opportunity to give of their *selves* to others who make some kind of demand on them. Let us now consider three principal ways in which a person can give: *giving possessions, giving in sex,* and *giving one's very self.*

First, one can *give possessions* by transferring something to another for the latter's use and enjoyment. How much one gives and shares will depend on the measure of love, the capacity to give, and the good or benefit that will come to the one loved. If the love is great, one will want to give all he has. The important thing is not the objective value of the gift but the subjective love with which it is given. As a result, lovers can become rich as persons because their giving is a personal sharing, not an impersonal charity.

Americans are well known for their generosity, yet some of the real motives behind their giving include tax deductions, status, recognition, return of a favor, expectations of a response, maintaining self-respect or reputation. Generosity with possessions requires that one be conscious of the needs of others — the problems of the poor, the ignorant, the deprived, the uneducated, the hopeless, and helpless.

Another type of giving, one that is intimately connected with love, is *giving in sex*. In true sexual union in marriage, the man and woman give themselves completely and totally to each other, body, mind, and soul. In giving one's body to another in love what is desired is union with that person, as well as joy, pleasure, and satisfaction for and with the partner. Obstacles to the ability to give oneself completely in sex are seen in homosexuality, masturbation, promiscuous sex, or sex for pleasure alone. Often these are symptoms of psychological problems.

The highest and most difficult, yet the most satisfying, form of giving, is *giving oneself* to others. What does a person give when one gives oneself? The giver shares something of what he or she is, one's life and that which is alive in oneself: joy and peace, interest and understanding, compassion and sympathy, knowledge and wisdom, wit and humor, talent and strength.

The more a person values the goodness of someone, the more he wants to safeguard this goodness. In the act of giving, he or she communicates personal joy, peace, tranquility, and courage, thereby putting his or her own qualities as a person at the service of the other.

This sharing of one's gifts and strengths is not itself love but a part of love. To love another in and for herself or himself is to affirm self in that person, and with self all the qualities of the lover's being. The giving of self according to the measure of one's love prompts him to give freely of his possessions and of his life without concern for gain or satisfaction; the beloved's gain or satisfaction becomes one's own. The other too becomes alive.

The giving which we have called love is not just a giving to someone for the sake of mere use and possession. It is a giving of oneself, a "self" who is somehow in the beloved because of this love. This mutual and true giving of self is interwoven with the minutest details of life shared with others; it does not just happen in the fleeting moments of a chance encounter or a temporary relationship. The amazing thing about all this is that most people can sense in their relationships those who give of themselves and those who, while friendly and kind, build up defenses against any entry into their personal lives. They seem afraid to love or to be loved.

Why don't people really give by opening themselves to others in love? The giving of self is exacting in its demands and difficult to achieve when set against the background of daily humdrum existence and the offhand way people meet and deal with one another. It requires a constant and deliberate effort to strive for unity and openness with others.

Many people are unable or unwilling to make the effort. Further, many are afraid to give themselves to others because in opening themselves up to another, there is always the possibility of getting hurt. This is to be expected in some relationships, but it must not be the reason to cut oneself off from others and to turn in on oneself. As the saying goes, "It is better to have loved and lost than never to have loved at all."

The greatest obstacle to giving oneself in love to someone is selfishness. If a person does not explicity and consciously orientate one's life toward others, one's love will be restricted to egoism. Loving only self, a person thinks of herself or himself, practically speaking, as an absolute, as the center of all actions. Others are treated simply as objects existing solely to be used.

Selfish love is so exclusive and slavish, restricted as it is within the narrow limits of self, that it never realizes its full potential nor the experience of liberation from the confines of individual life and self. The ego is washed back upon itself because it is unable to reach beyond self to others or to the plentitude of being, who is God. Thus the richness of others and of God himself are excluded from life, love, and experience.

The second way that love expresses itself is the *care and concern* people have for the life and growth of the persons they love. This care and concern should not be centered on one or a few intimates, but be as wide as the scope of our influence and contacts. If one is growing as a person, she or he begin to break out from the small circle of neighborhood or school friends who are much alike and move towards others who are different. A person feels a great deal more secure among people like oneself, but there is much to be learned from others, especially someone with a strong character and creative personality.

At first this reaching out to others may be disconcerting and discouraging, but it is the only thing that will help one grow out of narcissistic dreams of omnipotence and omniscience and acquire a genuine understanding and acceptance of self. At first a person may be overpowered by more competent people, but that is a necessary stage of growth. One must begin somewhere to widen the scope of one's care and concern. A person's love should begin to take on a universal quality.

"Do I really care about others? But what others? Am I really concerned about the needs of others? But what others? Am I really aware of others, their needs, their person, their problems? How wide is the scope of my love, my care, and concern? In practical terms, the answer to these questions demands that I must *act;* I must do something about it." As the motto of the Urban Coalition of New York puts it, "I must give a damn."

Now the attitudes of *care and concern* depend for their growth and development on what Fromm calls conditions or consequences of caring, namely: *knowledge* (consciousness), *responsibility, respect,* and (we will add another) *listening.*

To care for and to be concerned about another implies that one has knowledge and *consciousness* of the other — "to know you is to love you." To really know someone is to know that person as he or she really is. It means to penetrate the inner mystery and the secret of the other's being. It means to love their particular qualities. If one is really to know and love another as oneself, his or her qualities must be present to the lover in the same way that they are present to the other. This is not an easy thing to do. However, it is only through true knowledge of a person that one can understand him, penetrate the outer physical and psychic structure and reach the inner secret of his personhood.

Such understanding will help one distinguish another's physical and psychic characteristics — looks, actions, emotions, and desires — from the real self: attitudes, motives, and values. *It is in the act of loving, of giving oneself, in the act of penetrating the inner self of another, that one discovers oneself as of unique value and worth, one discovers the other, and one discovers both selves, and finally one discovers God.* In this way, one discovers one's relationship to fellow human beings and to God, the absolute unique value.

To care for and be concerned about others implies that one has a certain responsibility. If one cares and is concerned about others then a knowledge of others will lead one to *respond* to their physical, psychic, and spiritual needs expressed or unexpressed. Knowing the other, a person will be able to read the situation. Often a person's best response is simply a presence in time of need — loss, failure, tragedy, success, or joy. To understand how others feel and act, to open oneself to others in time of need or crisis are just a few ways to respond to others with care and concern. Responsibility is part of the human condition. Being human means being responsible, first to oneself and then to others. Thus human responsibility is the responsbility for the actualizing of potential values, one's own and others.

To care for and be concerned about others implies *respect* for others, the ability to see a friend as he is, not as one needs or wants him or her to be, as an object for one's use. To respect someone is to be aware of that person's unique individuality and worth. However, it would seem that respect for another is possible only when one has achieved independence oneself, standing alone without having to dominate or exploit anyone. Knowing oneself, being responsible for oneself and hence respecting oneself as a unique, independent person, one is able to respect everyone for what he is. The other demands by his or her very existence to be acknowledged as a person, as an "ego" in and for himself or herself. This is the claim which is implied in a person's very being, his "I am."

"I can refuse to listen; I can disregard his demands for justice and charity; I can remove, abuse, or use him; I can try to transform the other into a manageable object for my use, but in doing so I finally meet the resistance of him or her who has the claim to be acknowledged as an ego — as a person. And this very resistance forces me to meet the other as an independent ego."

Finally, to care for and to be concerned about others implies *listening* to others. *Love listens; this is its first task.* No kind of intimate human relationship is possible without listening. This is how one begins to know and to respect the other so that one does care and is concerned about others. There would be fewer reproaches, misunderstandings, quarrels, reactions, and defenses if there were more mutual listening among persons. Everybody calls out to others. Everybody wants to be listened to, to be understood in his intrinsic claims to a good life and true love. If a person cares and is concerned, he will develop a love which listens.

People can listen in all kinds of ways. Love uses all possible means to penetrate the deep place of another's motives, fears, attitudes, values, and inhibitions. Love listens, not just to speech, but to all kinds of human expressions which can mean something quite different from what they appear to be on the surface.

Seeming aggressiveness may be an expression of a love inhibited by shyness. Seeming sweetness and submission may actually be a symptom of repressed hostility. Everyone seems to have some type of physical or psychic hang up. *To love another is to let that person be himself or herself; to listen to her or him, to give the person the courage and encouragement to open up.* It is a sublime sort of confidence in life that dares to let whatever is be what it is. Ordinarily people imprison their fellowmen in stereotypes, which prescribe what they will permit others to be: "This person is conceited, that one is a loudmouth, a lot of people are such pains." But the person one judges to be conceited may be fighting bravely, if crudely, a lonely, painful, uphill battle for self-confidence; the person one takes to be a loudmouth may know no other way of making his or her needs audible; and all the people one overlooks may stand ironically as silent witnesses to one's own fear of revealing oneself. Those whom a person ignores are generally those who make him uncomfortable, and discomfort is evidence that beneath his self-declared superiority he feels threatened. Love that involves care and concern for others must learn to listen to all kinds of personal expressions, whether they are words, gestures, or actions. From *Desiderata* found on a wall plaque in St. Paul's Church in Baltimore we read, "Even the poor and the ignorant have something to say."

Conclusion

We started this chapter by examing ways in which man has attempted to define love. We finally centered our attention on such ideas of love as desire, presence, response, union, and affirmation. Using these basic ideas as being part of every love experience, we then proceeded to define love: *Love is a unifying response between two people who care for and have said "yes" to each other's total being. It presumes mutual acceptance of each other, freedom and trust, and it seeks the fulfillment and happiness of each other as a common goal.*

The dimensions of this definition were then seen in a discussion of love as desire and direct love. Such aspects as physical, psychic, and spiritual love helped clarify obscure concepts in the definition. Finally, in practical application of the definition two common ways in which love is experienced and expressed were discussed — love as giving and accepting, and love as care and concern. One theme that runs through the whole discussion of love is: a person must be able to stand as a mature individual before one can reach out to others as they are in themselves. This lengthy discussion of the mystery of love has given us enough material to evaluate ourselves on the quality of our own love.

While all this seems to complicate an almost universal experience, it can help us understand both its simplicity and complexity, with insights into how we can grow in love and improve our relationships with others. Just as grace is a seed of future glory, so love of others on this earth is a seed of a more perfect future union with God and mankind.

5

Christian Love—
What Is It?

Our search for meaning in love depends largely on the ideas we have about people: What are they all about? It is of equal importance in our search to know what ideas we have about God, especially as expressed by the Christian community: Who is he? What is he about? What is the relationship of people to God and vice-versa? Such statements as "God is Love" and "Where charity is, there is God" imply that human love somehow transcends the narrow limits of the physical and psychic world of people and reaches to the infinite. The statements that we have made about the human being as a unique individual, possessing dignity, value, and worth only make sense in terms of a life whose origin and destiny transcend purely physical and psychological existence.

To make sense out of love in terms of people, God, human destiny, we are forced to return to the age-old questions: "Who am I? Where do I stand in relation to others and to God? What is the point of what I am doing and where I am going? Can I live up to what is expected of me? What can I really do and why should I do it? What can I depend upon others to do? Could it be that God does exist and cares? What ought I to do with my life and why?"

We do not intend to take all these questions and answer them one by one; that would take another book. What we are trying to say is that the kind of love we have finally succeeded in defining makes no sense at all without acknowledging the existence of an absolute unique being whom we call God. Human worth and our dignity as unique beings follow from our sharing in God's own being. Through the bond of love, people see this same dignity in others; they see others the way God meant them to be. It has been said that to be fully Christian, one must at the same time be fully human. What, if anything, does Christianity add to human love?

At the center of Christian love is Jesus Christ. The God-man gives human history its fullest meaning. People freely charged by God with completing the work of love here on earth, yet understanding it little, needed a God more closely bound to human history and the human situation. A God-man who understood human life and love and could show people the way.

Therefore, the true meaning of God's creative love is to arrive at a human love capable of being united in and through Christ to divine love. It is Christ who demonstrated the transcendental power of human love and the possibility of its eventual and perfect fulfillment through union with divine love.

St. Paul states this fact well when he says, "If you love your fellow man, you have carried out your obligation. All the commandments: 'You shall not commit adultery, you shall not kill, you shall not steal, you shall not covet and so on, are summed up in the single command: You must love your neighbor as yourself.' Love is the only thing that cannot hurt your neighbor; that is why it is the answer to every one of the commandments" (Romans 13:8-10). Thus the whole of Christianity can be summed up by Christ's great commandment of love: the total love of God and the love of neighbor in the measure one loves oneself.

Christ's great commandment of love

Christ gave us the great commandments: "You must love the Lord your God with all your heart, with all your soul and with all your mind. You must love your neighbor as yourself" (Matthew 22:38-40). This commandment explicitly demands that everyone without exception love God totally and one's neighbor according to the measure of his or her own self-affirmation. This "measure" is fully explained by our definition. In the person-to-person relationships demanded by Christian love, one's individuality and uniqueness are preserved since people are to affirm the value and dignity of their own "self" as well as that of others — they affirm the self of others in the "measure" they affirm their own.

Thus people become both the subject and object of love. Further, Christ's commandment does not pick or choose or discriminate: Our love is to be universal, no one is to be excluded. Christian love, therefore, seeks to see others as God sees them: their *origin* in his creative love, their *value* as unique individuals worthy of love, their *dignity* as his sons and daughters, their need for *reconciliation, redemption,* and *saving grace* gained through his son's death and resurrection, and their *destiny* in eventual union with him by actual sharing in his divine life.

Being God's sons and daughters, we are all indeed brothers and sisters. If one actually believes this is the promise given to all people, one must begin to break the bubble of a self-centered world and move into the community of mankind. This is the demand of Christian love. Let us now take a closer look at the obligations that fall on us as Christians *to love self, to love neighbor* and *to love God.*

Love of self or *self-love* is natural self-affirmation and self-acceptance. In self-love a person values himself as God values him; he recognizes himself as possessing dignity and worth. The source of this dignity and worth is God himself. Christ's love was so great that he was moved to give the ultimate in love, his own life, to assure human, eternal destiny. Therefore what Christ gave human beings was dignity and worth, and this is the value that a person affirms when he loves himself.

Self-love is not selfishness; it is not a desire to draw all things and persons to oneself. At the root of selfishness is a misunderstanding of the true meaning of self. A person is not a closed-off or self-contained unit; one needs contact with others, the world, and God to discover and develop personality and personhood. As long as a person approaches others in a functional way as a tool, he closes himself off from the most powerful way for the self to emerge. There can be no separation comparable to the separation of a self-centered person from all other human beings. In such a person, there can be no real response to, union with, or affirmation of another because she or he has in effect split the "self." And since no one has within himself that which will totally fulfill him as a human being, such love will surely bring self-destruction.

By affirming oneself, a person also recognizes that everyone, by the fact of the origin and destiny of human beings, also shares dignity and worth. Thus one affirms others as unique persons of value all by themselves. The more one strives to be oneself, the more one enters into communion with others; it is through love alone that one comes to oneself, encounters oneself totally. This leads us to the next consideration: What is the love of neighbor?

Love of neighbor, according to the command of Christ, means that one loves another in the measure one loves oneself. *Affirming* another in the way one affirms himself or herself is to see that person as a sort of second self. For the other to be present, a person must not just see the other as an existing human being, as a variety of impersonal qualities and attributes that can be found equally in just anybody. One must somehow be *present* to that unique principle of action which the other is in himself or herself, so that he can *affirm* the other and *respond* to this discovery by giving love. Hence, love of neighbor looks beyond the physical and psychic characteristics to the source of being so that one can supply whatever is needed for the other's perfection and development.

It must be remembered that each of us expresses love in his or her own way. Loving response to one's neighbor implies that a person understand and listen to another's unique affirmation. In practical terms, to love a neighbor as oneself is to will the other good. A person gives to a neighbor because one loves her or him; one doesn't love the neighbor because one gives her or him something. If a neighbor is to be united with oneself, to love as one loves oneself, she or he will have to be so in her or his *otherness*. That unique trait or quality or attitude which separates the other from one must also unite the two — in the diversity there must be a communion of unique persons.

Let us not kid ourselves: to love a neighbor as oneself is not easy. One must leap over negative feelings towards other people, and this can be truly a leap in the dark. A person must let oneself go with a trusting confidence into the unknown reality of the other person, with faith in her or him, in the other's essential goodness as a human being, no matter what others say. When one presents himself in love to another, he reveals intimate and often vulnerable dimensions; and if rejected, he may be reluctant to love again unless he can be sure that the other will be accepting. Past failures in love may produce caution because one doesn't want to be hurt again. A person can easily get caught between desire and fear of love. People often wait for the other to open up and reveal himself or herself because they are afraid to take the initiative. In this situation a person could wait a lifetime, however. People must dare to believe in the reality and power of love.

True self-love and love of neighbor share in infinite love — God himself — which sustains us all and gives us the reason for existing. This leads us to the final consideration: love of God.

Love of God is a difficult reality to define and deal with, principally because of our past education and orientation in early youth. Yet experience tells us that many people, as they mature, become more aware of divine love, and for some people this becomes the overwhelming reality of their lives. Love for God in no way contradicts love for man. On the contrary, experience also suggests that the more one grows spiritually, the more one discovers that mutual human love is not only a gift of God's love but also a source of the depth and transcendence of love. What does all this mean?

The radical importance of love of neighbor and love of God can be seen from the following consideration. If a person cannot relate in a meaningful way to a neighbor in love, he cannot relate to the source of being in which all love becomes valid. If one can't love a friend, how can he love the source of the friend's ultimate origin and destiny, namely, God? Now the love of neighbor is not merely a condition, an effect, the fruit or touchstone of love of

God, but *love of neighbor is itself an act of this love of God*. It is an act within man's total surrender to God.

This is not just an idealist's claim; we have the words of St. John: "Anyone who fails to love can never have known God, because God is love. . . . Since God has loved us so much, we should love one another. No one has ever seen God; but as long as we love one another God will live in us and his love will be complete in us. . . . Anyone who says, 'I love God' and hates his brother, is a liar, since a man who does not love the brother that he can see cannot love God, whom he has never seen. So this is the commandment he has given us, that anyone who loves God must also love his brother . . . God who is love, has loved us, not so that we love him in return, but so that we love one another'' (1 John 4:7-21).

In other words, no one can say that he loves God if he treats neighbors as if they could not love or be loved by either God or others. Therefore, love of God and neighbor are the root of the whole Christian existence; love of neighbor really unites men and women with God since it is the all inclusive basic act of human existence.

Certain important ideas follow on this conclusion. The transcendental experience of God is possible only for a person who already has the human, concrete experience of true love of another. Relatedness to God is only given in experience with human beings. *God is not found or experienced apart from everyday experiences in life.* Love of neighbor is the primary act in which a person reaches the whole of reality, actualizes himself or herself and therein comes to the transcendental and immediate experience of God. When love of neighbor reaches its full depth, it is caught up and elevated by God's grace so that it is also love of God.

Christ tells us this through the words of Matthew: "I was hungry and you gave me food; I was thirsty and you gave me drink; I was a stranger and you made me welcome; naked and you clothed me, sick and you visited me, in prison and you came to see me. . . . Lord, when did I do all these things? . . . In so far as you did this to one of the least of these brothers of mine, you did it to me . . . and in so far as you neglected to do this to one of the least of these, you neglected to do it to me'' (Matt 25:36-46).

An analysis of Christian love

Love for God is really union with God, initially here on earth and finally in heaven. This love and union is a dynamic and growing reality. While the full realization and completion of love as union is bound to eternity and not to human beings and the world, people can and do do anticipate the kingdom of God here on earth through Christian love of others.

This statement is simple enough to understand, but how many people who call themselves Christians actually believe it and, what is more important, put it into practice? The difficulty in daily Christian living is that people fail to take the proper road to love because they are not seriously seeking to get insights into what love is. It is the opinion of Ignace Lepp in his book, *The Psychology of Loving:* "It is true that everybody everywhere talks about love. But the individuals who really know how to love are actually very rare. They are much rarer even than those who know how to think."

This is not encouraging. Worse still is the modern scandal of those who call themselves Christians and really aren't; their lives just don't show it. They really don't know Christ, the man who suffered for us and is still in our midst today; they really don't live Christianity in their daily lives. *If Christ really is, this fact should make a difference in their daily lives, not just on Sundays.* Our considerations here have given us enough to think about, to evaluate the quality of our love; it is now necessary to do something about it.

In summary: we participate in God's existence, being, and value; hence, our love as well as our dignity and worth as human beings are rooted in the divine life — in something which transcends our temporal life both in being and meaning. This sharing in the divine life is made possible by God himself who sent his son to reopen the path to union through grace, the sacraments and above all a life lived in love. The love of others is a reflection of our love of God, since all people are one with us in the divine life of God. The tremendous love of God for people is realized in every individual — Christ came to save us as individuals, as unique persons in and for ourselves. No matter what our personalities and characters, our strengths and weaknesses, we have dignity, value, and worth as sons and daughters of God and, being such, heirs also to the kingdom of God. This is the promise given to every human being. It is in value, and worth in recognition of this dignity ourselves and our fellow human beings that we love one another as brothers and sisters. This is the true meaning of Christian Love.

6

Love: Some Conclusions

Our search for the meaning of love has shown us that love is a dynamic reality which will continue to unfold both here and hereafter. Whatever else love is, it is creative; it continually seeks new ways to express itself. This is the power and energy of love. Once we come to know and love a person, he or she begins to reveal a new depth or inner core that never ceases to amaze. That is why we can never stereotype persons: Our relationships would die.

We started this section by examining our attitudes toward love. Is it an art or a happening? After concluding that love is an art requiring knowledge and effort, we proceeded to evaluate ways in which people attempt to achieve union to escape separateness and aloneness. We found that none of these ways, though satisfying human needs, could be considered love. Whatever way people love, they must do so as independent individuals. Using this fact as a base, we then centered on the ideas of desire, joy, response, union, and affirmation as necessary to love. We described the two dimensions of love — love as desire and direct love — as well as the two expressions of love — love as giving-accepting and love as care and concern. Thus completing our discussion of love as a human reality, we tried to see what Christianity added to love.

We concluded that the uniqueness, worth, and dignity of every individual, implied by our definition of love, made sense only in terms of human origin in the creative act of God and human destiny in union with God. Thus affirming this value first in themselves, people also affirm it in their neighbors. This is what is implied in the great commandment of Christ. Taking the words of the commandment, we attempted to find the meaning of love of self, neighbor, and God. We ended the discussion with an analysis of Christian love in terms of the unity of all people in God through Christ.

BIBLIOGRAPHY

Note: The books listed here and in Sections Two and Three were used as references in preparing the sections. The books marked with an asterisk (*) are fairly easy reading and are recommended if you wish to pursue the topics further. The others are good books, but some of them may be tough reading.

Buber, Martin. *I and Thou,* trans. by R.G. Smith. New York: The Scribner Library, 1958. (paperback)
Chauchard, Paul. *Teilhard de Chardin on Love and Suffering.* Glen Rock, N.J.: Paulist Press, 1966. (paperback)
Frankl, Viktor E. *The Doctor and the Soul.** New York: Bantam Books, Inc., 1967. (paperback)
—————— . *Man's Search for Meaning.** New York: Washington Square Press, Inc., 1963. (paperback)
Fromm, Erich. *The Art of Loving.** New York: Bantam Books, Inc., 1960. (paperback)
Guitton, Jean. *Human Love.* Chicago, Ill.: Franciscan Herald Press, 1966.
Johann, Robert O. *Building the Human.* New York: Herder and Herder, 1968.
—————— . *The Meaning of Love.* Glen Rock, N.J.: Paulist Press, 1966. (paperback)
Lepp, Ignace. *The Psychology of Loving.** Trans. by Bernard B. Gilligan. New York: The New American Library, 1963. (paperback)
Marcel, Gabriel. *Men Against Society.** Chicago, Ill.: Henry Regnery Co., 1962. (paperback)
Mouroux, Jean. *The Meaning of Man.* New York: Image Books (Doubleday), 1948. (paperback)
Oraison, Marc. *Love or Constraint.* Glen Rock, N.J.: Paulist Press, 1961. (paperback)
Rahner, Karl. "The Unity of Love of God and Love of Neighbor." *Theology Digest,* Vol. XV, No. 2, 1967.

Scripture Quotations are taken from: *Jerusalem Bible.* Garden City, N.Y.: Doubleday and Co. Inc., 1966.

Tillich, Paul. *Love, Power, and Justice.** New York: Oxford University Press, 1960. (paperback)

Toner, Jules. *The Experience of Love.* Washington, D.C.: Corpus Books Inc., 1968.

van Kaam, Adrian, Croonenburg, Bert, and Muto, Susan A. *The Emergent Self.** Wilkes-Barre, Pa.: Dimension Books Inc., 1968.

Watkins, Aelred. *The Enemies of Love.** Glen Rock, N.J.: Paulist Press, 1965. (paperback)

What Meaning Exists in Sex and Sexuality?

7

Sex: A Discussion of the Question

Our culture seems to be more preoccupied with sex than with other aspects of life. This overemphasis may be a symptom of the inability of modern society to integrate sex into the totality of life. Such a process is a lifelong task and implies that people live in a world of sexual meaning, that many possibilities of sexual fulfillment are offered in everyday life. Since people are free, they can decide for themselves to what degree and in what manner they will respond sexually. If a person learns to integrate sex into existence in a wholesome way, her or his personal answer to the sexual appeal of the world will be compatible with the whole orientation of life.

It is a consensus in modern American society that people should develop a better understanding of sex and sexuality. Sex is seen to be a fundamental dimension of human existence, and people cannot continue to avoid the major sex question that many young people get hung up on. It is a fact of daily experience that the first thing a person notices when he meets someone is the other person's sex, and this in turn affects the consequent relationship.

Unfortunately, adolescents receive little authentic and practical information about sex, in or out of school. Adults usually talk over, under, and around it but not at it. What little information is made available to teenagers usually consists of depersonalized accounts of the physiology of sex with a combination of do's and don't's. This approach has little effect on attitudes or actions. And the commercialized information received in some stores and street corners only compounds the confusion.

This gap in sex education is not just on the biological side. When young people have frank and direct sex education, they are better prepared to meet the challenges and freedom of the adult life opening up to them. They have not only knowledge but, what is more important, a set of values, attitudes, and morals for sound decision-making in sex. Certainly if they are to become responsible parents, they must first develop responsible attitudes toward sex when they are young.

For the most part, Christianity has consistently worked to elevate sex and sexuality to the level of a positive and desirable good. It has tried to encourage a strong monogamous family life, to foster through self-control a direction for the sexual appetite, to recognize woman as man's equal, to enhance the education and development of children. These have been part of the Church's tradition. Yet sexual values, customs and the institution of marriage are being affected by the changing attitudes toward sex and morality in today's society. Issues included are such things as the stability of marriage, family planning, premarital sex, dating patterns, the roles and relationships of man-woman, wife-husband and mother-father, laws governing contraception, adultery, sterilization, abortion, child care, and child education.

This section will consider the place of sex and sexuality in the total personality and life of a human being. *The basic thesis is that sex affects the total person, not just his physical relations with others.* No other instinct in a person has greater implications for his or her life than does the sex instinct. First, we will consider the instincts in human beings, and the sex instinct in particular, to see how they affect the person and personality. Next, we will study sex from the viewpoint of moral integrity, especially as it applies to young people. Finally, we will examine some of the obstacles to sexual maturity that are found in culture today. Emphasis will be put on how sex can be integrated with love as a preparation for marriage.

8

Instincts in Man: A Positive Good

There is much physiological and psychological confusion about the sex instinct. That the sex drive and its consequent sexual desire and arousal are a real part of our lives is the common experience of everyone. That this drive, desire, and arousal can be brought into operation by a multitude of physical and psychological stimuli is also a fact of experience. Yet when the sex drive makes its appearance in the adolescent personality at puberty, it is not yet a psychological reality but merely the adolescent's reaction to a physical event for which he or she may not be prepared. Research also has shown that sex interest is not asleep from ages six to twelve. Further, sex and sexuality are influenced by upbringing, social pressure, personal needs, and early sex education.

At puberty sexual desire has not yet been shaped by the personality or integrated into the life of the person. At this stage, young people are aware of sexual desire but are not ready as full human beings to express themselves completely in a love relationship. Little by little however, the adolescent begins to respond to the sexual fact of puberty by attempting to understand his psycho-sexual desires. As one develops and matures psychologically, physically, and morally, the sex instinct moves the person to a fulfilling human relationship.

Let us now clear up some of the confusion about the sex

drive by discussing the source of this drive, which is the sex instinct itself.

Instincts in general

There is a difference of opinion about the specific nature of an instinct. Freud, talking about the sex instinct, called it the basic life force in man from birth to death — the will to pleasure (libido). Modern evidence has shown Freud's theory to be much too narrow to answer the psychological and spiritual questions arising from sex. Without taking time to discuss all the modern theories, we will center our attention on one that makes good sense and is accepted by many people today.

What are the instincts? Certain physiological organs are grouped together in a system whose activating, dynamic, and vital element is called an instinct. All the organs working together in a system need to function properly to be satisfied. The instincts assure that the system or organs will be brought into operation.

For example, hunger is the result of the proper functioning of that system of organs from the mouth to the anus involved in digestion. It is not just the stomach or any other single organ but the whole digestive system working together that brings on hunger. These organs are satisfied by the proper functioning of the hunger instinct, and this satisfaction is accompanied by pleasure. Instincts, then, are basically bodily powers.

Of themselves instincts are blind powers; of themselves they have little or no direction. The instincts tend to be satisfied where and how they will. Further, the abuse of nature causes nature to impose sanctions; therefore, the instincts in men and women cannot be abused or repressed without retaliation from nature. The instincts must be directed if they are to be truly human.

What are the instincts for? Generally, the instincts are directed to maintaining the individual in physical existence with proper balance. Except for the sex instinct, failure to respond to the urge of the instincts often endangers life itself. For example, if a person refuses to eat, he or she will die. Therefore, both the origin and the end of the instincts is the individual. The physical needs of the individual are expressed and realized by means of this dynamism of the instincts.

Instincts are a dynamic part of the animal world, but there is a great *difference between instincts in animals and in human beings*. While the first movements of the instincts in both are the same, the influence on further acts is radically different. In animals the instincts are determined as to purpose and function. They are directed by nature so that the individual animal as well as the species will be maintained in existence.

In human beings, however, the instincts are not separate from the whole person. We are not only physiological beings, but spiritual and psychological beings. For this reason it is necessary for people, through education and self-discipline, to put direction into instincts so that they will be integrated into the totality of life; otherwise people remain slaves of their drives and urges. The eternal striving of human beings is to rise above purely physical existence, to free themselves of the blind demands of instincts. This means trying to love as whole human beings, striving to reach our potential, integrating our physiological, spiritual, and psychological natures.

Like all instincts, the sex instinct is rooted in human physical life. It originates from a cooperation among organs in a system making up the sex organs: the endocrine glands and their hormones, the sexual glands and their hormones, the nervous system, and the internal and external sex organs themselves. These organs working together in a system actuate the sex instinct which gives an impulse to satisfy the instinct. The instinct awakens in the sensuous nature of a man or woman the impulse toward a physical sex act that gives sexual satisfaction. Such an act results in pleasure and the satisfaction of the sex instinct. This awakening of the instinct, also called sexual arousal, is usually signalled by the erection of the sex organ in the male and vaginal secretions in the female, so that sexual union is both possible and desirable. As such, arousal is both natural and good.

It is to be noted that any organ in the sexual system may be stimulated to bring on sexual arousal. Thus, the stimulus can be either psychic or physical: a thought, a picture, a person, a physical touch, a movement, or a contact. Even organs in close contact with the sex organs may bring on arousal. For example, a man may wake up in the morning with a penis erect because of the close proximity of a full bladder to the male internal sex organs. Sexual arousal is not always a conscious operation but a bodily reaction to a stimulus. Men's experiences with embarrassing erections are an example of this.

The strength of the sex instinct is an individual thing differing with each person, male and female. In men, for instance, it is usually strong in adolescence and becomes weaker with age. In most women the sex instinct awakens slowly and becomes stronger with age. This is not to say it isn't present to some degree earlier. While a woman may try to keep her feelings in check, she cannot ignore what is happening to her body. For many girls, the desire is very strong.

What is the purpose of the sex instinct in people?

The sex instinct and consequent sexual arousal in people is not evil or dirty but a good, necessary, and pleasant sensation. Physically, the union of the sexes is designed for the meeting and fusion of the complementary cells (male sperm and female ovum) in such a way that reproduction results. The sex instinct then impels a person to play a part in reproduction within the species.

From a very narrow physiological point of view, there is no other reason for the existence of the sexual function. However, as we shall discuss in later chapters, the sexual function plays a larger very important role in terms of the total human personality. It acts as a powerful force affecting the psychological and spiritual union of a man and woman. Depending on how it is used in their lives, the sexual relationship of a man and woman may either marvelously enrich or totally debase their union.

Unlike the other instincts, the sex instinct transcends the

individual and has as its final goal the continuation of the human species. Its individual exercise is not necessary, and those who do not use it suffer no harm. Despite stories one may hear, there is no harm in abstinence. However, the misuse of sex usually has harmful psychological and moral effects.

Because of its origin and operation, the *sex instinct in people can be a source of problems or enrichment* – depending on how it is used. The voluntary and free character of human activities implies that people must give definite *direction* to their instinctive, emotional and voluntary forces. Human beings are free to direct their sexual life toward goals of which they must be at least implicitly aware. What we are saying is that no sexual activity which eludes the direction of free will can be termed human; it remains on the instinctive level.

The sex instinct must be allowed to grow and develop to become normal and healthy during adolescence. Recent research shows that the sexual upbringing of the child determines, to some extent, the later course of his sexual development. It seems likely that the sex instinct is influenced by social pressures as well as personal needs and opportunities for finding out about sex. Unreasonable and ill-timed do's and don't's in early childhood can easily turn into psycho-sexual problems during adolescence and later life.

Playing with oneself, sexual curiosity, and discovery are natural phenomena of childhood. When a parent sees a child playing with his genitals, what better time to say, "Mike, that's called your penis" or "Genevieve, that's your vagina." Distracting the child's attention could lead the child to interpret it as something that should not be done around parents. Letting the child discover himself is good. Explanations during this self-discovery will help the child develop and understand his or her sexual nature. Some examples: "That opening (urethra) is for urine to flow out so your body keeps in good working order."

The early needs of the child have to be satisfied in a healthy way and not repressed. Early conflicts lead to frustration which must be satisfied by some compensation. Whatever the compensation, it should be natural and healthy. For example, some psychologists talk about the "Oedipus" stage in a child's life. Oedipus, King of Thebes, slew his father and married his mother. In the Oedipus stage of a child's life, a conflict arises when the boy wishes to possess his mother exclusively or the girl wishes to possess her father exclusively. The other parent becomes a rival and a challenge, and the child often becomes hostile to this parent. He or she may learn to play a game with affection by giving it to the one while denying it to the other. If the game does not succeed, frustration may set in, and the child begins to compensate, often in immature sexual ways. Though some psychologists dismiss the theory, parents should be aware that similar problems do exist. The solution to these early sexual problems involving the sex instinct is to be found in the love and affection of parents for each other and for their children. Unity of parents is essential to healthful sex education.

The sex instinct is especially strong in early adolescence, and the instinct is almost entirely without direction because its integration into the whole person is still developing. The inclination is toward satisfaction, depending on opportunity and chance. This process should not be repressed; rather the person must learn to view it as part of his or her total being, including other needs, goals, and values. Conflict between the adolescent's high ideals, values, and morals on the one hand and the strength of her or his sex instinct and an accompanying curiosity about it on the other hand, leads to a feeling of frustration. Not knowing how to cope with the situation, the adolescent may compensate for the frustration growing out of the conflict by masturbation, the self-manipulation of the sex organs to the point of orgasm. Self-gratification through masturbation usually releases the tensions built up by the sex instinct. If the conflict continues, the practice may become an obsessive habit. Society's view of such practices often leads to adolescents' withdrawal from those who can help the most, especially parents and counsellors. And masturbation often brings on feelings of guilt. For many, these are probably feelings of failure resulting from hurt pride or loss of control rather than feelings of guilt resulting from sin.

Bernard Haring in his book *Shalom: Peace* says, "It would be contrary to tradition, of course, to maintain that masturbation is never a mortal sin or to claim it is almost never a sin." On the other hand, he agrees that enlightened advice and counsel should be given young people concerning this practice so as to help them work through it effectively, without creating further psychological problems either at present or in the future. It should be noted that there is a moral as well as a psychological dimension to masturbation, and this will be discussed later (see Chapter 12).

Conclusion: The sex instinct in people

The sex instinct in people is an impulse activated by the system of sex organs. As a source of sexual arousal, it is an impulse to physical sexual satisfaction, resulting in pleasure. This impulse and consequent arousal, satisfaction, and pleasure are both good and necessary. The end sought by this biological instinct in human beings, however, is neither the existence of the individual nor the pleasure of the physical union, but the preservation of the species.

In people the sex instinct becomes truly human when it is integrated into the psychological and spiritual love between a man and a woman. The sex instinct is not just a blind power under nature's command but a power subject to the will. Every sexual act by people should be a human act which involves the whole person. The sexual urge found in the sex instinct can be developed into truly human sexual response.

Thus a young person has begun to understand and control the sexual instinct, moving it from a purely physical urge to that of a positive directed force in his or her total personality. The young adult has given it meaning to the degree that it has become ordered through love. This psycho-sexual maturity of the individual is possible only, however, if there has first been self-discipline and concern for others learned in early life. The young girl or boy who has learned some self-discipline that makes him or her thoughtful of self and of others is much more apt to grow into a young adult for whom sexuality has real meaning — as an expression of unselfish love.

9

Sex and Sexuality: Human Meanings and Implications

The word *sex* is used to mean almost anything of a sexual nature. In modern literature the word *sexuality* has crept into the vocabulary, only to add to the confusion: What is sex? What is sexuality? How are they related? This chapter will attempt to answer these questions and discuss the meaning and implication of sex and sexuality in our lives.

Sex and sexuality: What are they and how are they related?

In this book, the word *sex* is generally used to refer to the physical and biological aspects of the sex instinct, the sex organs, and their physical operation. Sex includes not only the primary male and female sex characteristics but also the secondary sex characteristics.

Sexuality, on the other hand, is used to refer to the psychic and spiritual aspects of the sex instinct — the function of sex in human life. Sexuality refers to the constitution and life of the individual as related to sex and its effect on the total personality. Sexuality is the human personality as expressed in the sexual area. The implication here is that sex has been integrated into human life and as such helps perfect the person. Human sexuality is complex because it includes all elements of the total personality. Sexuality never appears as a merely physiological phenomenon in a man or a woman; it also includes the psychic and spiritual aspects of a person.

A positive good

Sex has a meaning for human life. A person's attitude toward sex is of greater significance for her or his personality and development as a mature individual than any other human instinct. Sex has a depth that other bodily pleasures do not possess, both as to the nature and intensity of the sexual acts.

Sexual ecstasy goes to the depth of bodily existence. It is truly an extraordinary power and energy. Unlike the other instincts, sex has an intimacy, an attraction, a mystery, a secret character, a fascination, and an effect on one's whole life and attitudes. It is no wonder that the act of sexual intercourse is called the perfect physical expression of mutual love. Because of its significance, it tends to be incorporated with experiences of a higher order that are purely psychological or spiritual. These experiences and attitudes are what we have termed sexuality, the function of sex in a person's life. In marriage, sex and sexuality are the basic source of growth in love and grace.

The more one develops the psychological and spiritual aspects of oneself, the more meaning and satisfaction sex generates. On the other hand, if one does not respond sexually as a whole person, sex finds immature expressions and results in dissatisfaction. Sex becomes an integrated part of human life, as a person grows and matures. While in the beginning of sexual awakening any partner might satisfy the sex instinct, the sexual urge must gradually be aim-directed. Because it is blind, the sex instinct leads the immature person to selfishness, to non-integrating love, to non-commitment, rather than to true altruism (other-directedness). Therefore, a person must direct the sex instinct and its expression to a meaningful love relationship. Failure in this regard leads a person to seek satisfaction selfishly in masturbation or in incomplete sex, such as homosexuality and lesbianism.

In early, and even in late adolescence, these acts of selfish or incomplete sex may occur because of the ready availability of a sex object — first oneself, then maybe a friend. It isn't until dating takes place on a regular basis that sex involves first girls or boys in general and then a girl or a boy in particular. It is no accident that steady dating is a normal part of the modern social pattern. The desire to center one's love on one person is a natural outcome of a developing maturing personality.

Sexuality has a meaning in people's lives.

People have to live their lives not only as individuals but also as members of a community made up of men and women. Despite the tendency of some people in society to consider sex and sexuality as dirty or evil and others to center on the playboy or playgirl ideal of sex, sexuality is a positive physical, psychic, and social good in people's lives. There will always be those unfortunate persons who misunderstand and misuse sex in their lives. The human being who is happiest and has reached the fullest potential, however, is the one who has made sexuality a positive good in life.

As a physical good, sexuality is a creative act between a man and a woman in marriage. It is the power to carry love and sexual union between two persons to the point of creating new life. Propagation of life has meaning only when and if life itself represents something meaningful. Therefore, the sex instinct is a distinct impulse to creative love. Men and women who love each other instinctively desire to express this through the physical sex act. In doing so they enhance and solidify their mutual love, union and harmony. This act of total physical love becomes a beautiful symbol or way of expressing in their lives what their love means to them — a total giving of each to the other. Sexual acts that play this role in people's lives are natural, necessary, and good. Here the sex act plays an intimate part in revealing what it means to be a man or a woman. Its object is to give complete sexual fulfillment and pleasure to the other as well as physically to express the psychological and spiritual union of their lives.

Some think the sex function tends to dominate the life of a

woman more than that of the man. Typical of this view is Lord Byron's line, "man's love is of a man's life, a thing apart/ Tis woman's whole existence." On the other hand, if we take a hard look at the Playboy culture we also see the sex function dominating the life of the man. Here we might rightfully conclude that the male is dominated by the sex function because he seems to need the self image of the sexual conqueror to bolster his misguided male ego. It is true that historically women's lives have been taken up much more totally with sex through motherhood; however this aspect of woman's life is changing rapidly. What is needed today is a reappraisal of men's and women's attitudes towards each other that will accord with a higher conception of each other as persons, not as sexual objects or tools to provide security or reinforce egos. While most of these attitudes are cultural, part of the reason for them might have been that a man's physical concern in the sexual relationship ended where a woman's just began, in the advent of motherhood. Today it is different. Rapidly changing views of family size and the place of women in society are forcing a reappraisal of the male and female function in physical sex and sexuality as well. What lies ahead is the realignment of the demands that marriage and the home will make upon men and women.

The women's liberation movement has paved the way for a discovery on the part of women of how they can better use their talents in our society. A closer look, though, will reveal that men also are frozen in stereotyped roles in our society. The coming generation will see each sex faced with problems in finding new roles. Sexuality more than ever will have to assume meaning in people's lives.

Sexuality is also a *psychic good* — a total donation of self to another. From what has just been said about the physical aspects of sexuality, it is easy to see that a person can easily give his or her body to another in sex and from this to get pleasure. But what does it mean to give and share one's body, mind, and soul in sex? What, if anything, does the psychic aspect of sex add to the enjoyment of sex? Is there a difference between having sex with a prostitute, or any male or female, and with someone in a love relationship? Sexual self-completion can only be had through true mutual sexual self-donation and acceptance: a person giving herself or himself — body, mind, and soul — totally to another and receiving the other totally. The sex partner must know that there is more being given and shared than the other person's sex organs. What is desired is union with someone who is loved; and sex is a sign, symbol, and expression of this love and union, the desire to be one with the other. *Such psychic attitudes definitely heighten the enjoyment of the sex act.* If precedence is given to sensual satisfaction, however, the biological and psychological make-up of people brings about a resurgence of egocentricity. Sex becomes less than human. What started as real love and self-donation ends up only as pleasure seeking and selfishness.

One can test his sexual psychic growth by honestly answering a few questions:

"What do I look for on a date? Why do I make out? Why do I kiss, neck, and pet? How much of what I do with my partner has real meaning and is expressive of my love and a sign of my affection and concern for the other? Or how much of what I do is of a purely selfish nature?"

Sexuality is also a *social good,* a total mutual commitment to and with another. The sexual function in people is social in that it is a mutual sharing of sex with another. The specific social goods of human sexuality are the human beings that may result from this sharing of sex. Thus, people have within themselves the power to create a community of persons for which they are responsible. This community is theirs to influence and to instruct in their own values, principles, and ideas. Thus as a social good, sexuality implies a total commitment of body, mind, and soul to another which finds satisfaction in marriage and in a home. The problem is that this commitment can be temporary and not total. It depends in great part on whether one has developed a monogamous attitude toward sex and sexuality: "Can I really be satisfied by one person for a lifetime?"

The next problem brought up was the *male and female personalities*. No man is complete in his masculinity or a woman in her femininity. People conjure up ideas for themselves of what constitutes the ideal man or woman. Every human being, consciously or unconsciously, lacks security with regard to complete sexualization. In most people there is a gap between one's *physical sex* (male or female sex organs) and psychological sex (what makes a male or female in our society). The *psychic image* people have of themselves is seen in feelings of adequacy or inadequacy in the sexual area that affect relationships with others. The psychic image people have of themselves gives rise to a *body image* — what they think of themselves physically as males or females. Body image lends itself to all kinds of psychological hang-ups.

Some men become hung-up on such things as penis size, hair distribution on their bodies, looks, body size, and muscle structure. However serious hang-ups don't occur in men who have healthy concepts of themselves and others as valuable persons. Problems of chronic impotence, transvestism, homosexuality, and other related sexual problems seem to reflect a basic disorientation of the total personality with that of the opposite sex. Strongly focused concern of a person about his own physical sexual characteristics is a sign of a deeper personal turmoil. A man who is unsure of his male personhood may try to demonstrate masculinity by turning into a playboy or a Don Juan "lover."

Some women become hung-up on such things as breast size, body measurements, weight and beauty. Ordinary concern about these things are common in our culture which emphasizes beauty and attractiveness in women. It is only when deep feelings of personal inadequacy are present that women tend to focus on these aspects of themselves in a destructive way. A woman who is deeply troubled about her feminine personhood may develop such problems as chronic frigidity, lesbianism, or prostitution. A woman who is insecure about herself may try to find feminity by becoming a mere sexual tool or by over-emphasizing her sexual endowments in dress and appearance.

One's body image forms what we will call one's *identity* or *self-concept* — what image people think they project to others. This image is what people think of themselves as male or female *persons* as revealed through their physical selves. This self-concept affects one's *role identity* as female or male, wife or husband, mother or father.

Today, more than ever before, women and men are confronted directly and deeply with their own sexuality. Changing structures and patterns of family, culture, society, work, and groups make definition of roles more difficult. Society defines roles for its individuals. People can usually act out a role until they adjust to it. Thus, for example, if the roles of husband or father are well-defined by the culture and clearly transmitted by a parent figure a man can get married and act out the role as defined by society until such times as he has created these roles for himself. However, when role definition becomes unclear and is criticized, then problems in role identity appear. This confusion affects one's self-concept, and self-identity definitely affects sex-identity. Adverse results may be masturbation, homosexuality, lesbianism, impotence, and frigidity. The question of what is the female or male identity in our society becomes a problem for many, especially in the area of personality. Such magazines as Playboy and Playgirl add to the confusion of the male and female identities in their one-dimensional representations of sexuality.

At this point we must emphasize that individuals can be creative in living secure male or female roles in our society despite growing problems of role definition all around them. The determining factor as to whether or not an individual will be able to do this is his experience in early life. Two things are always present in a young adult's experience. First, experience has already taught whether or not he or she is a valuable person worthy of self respect; secondly, he or she has spent most of life experiencing in the home what it means to be a man or a woman, a husband and father, a wife and mother. The learning process has had an enduring effect on the way this person will interpret roles. Depending on that home life, the young man or woman may be confused, be totally secure, or be mixed up about the meanings of particular roles. In accord with that person's inner personal strength and security, future role definition may be approached in a very rigid fearful way or in a flexible creative way. A young man and woman beginning marriage together can work out loving and mutually fulfilling roles if they are equipped with enough inner strength to be flexible and creative, with enough common sense to adapt what they have already learned, and with enough love to want to do so.

It is assumed that males and females are different, and not only physically. This is a controversial point. There is no doubt that many of the differences between males and females are the result of environment, upbringing, and culture. The fact was certainly implied when we discussed self-image and role definition. Yet despite the tremendous effect that culture has on the development of the male-female personality, there is evidence that males and females are basically different.

This is concluded from the fact that their physical differences are only the outward sign of a fundamentally deeper difference. What man can know or feel what it means to be a woman, to bear children, or to respond sexually as a woman? What woman knows what a man feels and thinks and endures? The basic physical differences are bound to affect the psychic and spiritual life of a person. Knowing these basic differences will help one form an identity or self-image that will transcend the cultural changes in role definition that are going on today.

Implications of sex and sexuality

Having defined sex and sexuality and discussed their meaning for people, we must now ask ourselves what are the implications? The first implication would seem to be a person's obligation to realize fully his or her sexual potential. To do this, one must gain some degree of sexual maturity. One must also develop mature, heterosexual relationships in and out of marriage and be able to relate to persons of the opposite sex in a meaningful and healthy way. Finally, the whole problem of sex and sexuality is intimately connected with love.

What is sexual maturity and how is it attained?

Simply stated, sexual maturity is the healthy integration of sex and sexuality into the totality of one's life. Anyone who has achieved a degree of maturity as a man or woman has also achieved a degree of sexual maturity. Specifically, it involves one's basic attitudes toward the opposite sex and one's orientation toward establishing sexual values, ideals and mores in one's personal life. Sexual meaning in one's life depends in great part on the meaning one puts on the male or female identity. Everyone has some sexual values operating in her or his life and these values grow and develop out of one's self-concept as female or male. No one's sex life operates independently of sexual values.

How is maturity obtained? Growth of the total personality and character together with growth in love results in a corresponding growth in the sex instinct and the sexual function in human life. Sex practices and attitudes in adolescence have a direct bearing on the ability to achieve sexual harmony later on in marriage. Selfishness and self-centeredness are the main obstacles to sexual growth.

That a man or a woman lives as a sexed individual implies that he or she must develop healthy *heterosexual relationships* in and out of marriage, that is, he or she must give *direction* to the sex instinct. As free beings, people have the power to build individual personal being and a community. Giving direction to the sex instinct is a matter of *developing relationships* between persons of the opposite sex, rather than merely coming together instinctively. Therefore, sex requires a *relational attitude,* an altruistic (other-directed) attitude.

This just doesn't happen; people have to work at it. Often they lead lives in expectation of what is to come rather than in fulfillment resulting from present human relationships. To live in future expectation is not to live at all. Sexuality, then, is a matter of developing human relationships now — day to day.

Sex and love: How are they related? The attraction between men and women becomes love when all the forces of body, mind, and spirit come together in mutual self-growing. In all cases, love is in control — sex being but one means of its expression. Sexuality must involve the power of love. The stronger the power of love and the deeper it penetrates two persons, the more they will be able to direct their sex instinct and involve themselves totally.

Conclusion: sex and sexuality

It is obvious from what has been said in this chapter about the meaning and implication of sex and sexuality that many people do not achieve the degree of maturity necessary for sex to be an integrating force in their lives. To live one's life as a sexed person is easier to say than to do. One must have a clear ideal of his or her male or female identity to live life in healthy relationships with persons of the same or opposite sex. When one's self-concept is clear and precise, a person is free to direct the sex instinct to its proper purpose. In other words, a person cannot give what he or she does not possess — in this case, a self. This means there must be a certain growth and maturity in the total personality.

When people have identity problems, they often end up with sexual problems. Self-identity can be equated with sex identity. The lack of a clear and personally acceptable self-image can lead to homosexuality, lesbianism, sex for pleasure alone, masturbation, impotence, frigidity, and other sorts of undirected and misdirected sex practices. This chapter has attempted to put into focus the necessity of integrating the physical aspects of sex with the psychic and the spiritual.

10

The Function of the Sex Organs

A common source of misunderstanding between the sexes, either during dating and later courtship or in marital life, arises from basic differences between male and female sexual activity and sexual responses and resulting sexual behavior. This problem is reflected in the statement of Dr. Mary Calderone, the executive director of the Sex Information and Educational Council of the United States, when she says, "Boys are ready for sex and not for love. Girls are ready for love and not for sex."

The adolescent and adult male frequently does not understand how sex appears to a girl or woman, what her attitudes are, or upon what basis her sexual responsiveness or lack of responsiveness rests.

A sexually aroused boy can easily misinterpret a girl's sigh as a sigh of passion or a yes because he thinks the girl reacts as he does. Similarly, the girl is often unable to comprehend what sex means to the boy and how and when he responds sexually to stimuli so that she is unable to gain an insight into his point of view or reaction. A girl may know that she can get a boy easily aroused by allowing him certain freedoms and she may play upon this because she looks upon it as a power that she has over him or as a sign of his affection. In reality, she is playing a game with him by dangling sex in front of him and not realizing what effect it has on him. Likewise, boys often take advantage of girls by demanding certain freedoms under the pretense or expressions of love. The more women can learn about the male and his sexual responsiveness and the more men can learn about the female response, the greater the chance they can work out compatible dating relationships that will eventually lead to successful courtship and marriage. It may help to solve the sexual hang-ups that most couples are subject to today in dating.

Books on adolescent behavior often stress the fact that girls are a year or so ahead of boys in physical, emotional, social and intellectual growth and development, and that boys don't catch up until the late teens or early twenties. This is generally not true in sexual growth and sexual response. Usually there is a big gap between male and female sexual development and response with the girl lagging behind the boy.

When general statements are made about sexual development in young people, particularly when comparisons are made, it must be remembered that such statements do not necessarily apply to every boy and girl in exactly the same way. The main point is that sexual development is different for boys and girls, and that their sexual needs are different, a difference that usually is not understood by the opposite sex. A general knowledge of sexual development, with due allowance for variations in individual persons, will help young people understand one another better.

Unlike girls, whose sexual awakening is usually slow but progressive, boys after puberty have experienced at least some orgasms. Charged with an urgent sex drive, boys after puberty may be frequently aroused sexually with erections, almost to the point of embarassment, and they may experience considerable sexual activity through wet dreams or masturbation. Girls of the same age are often relatively unresponsive as far as sex is concerned. Thus boys often bring more sexual experience to dating than do girls. This might be the reason why many girls don't realize what they are doing when they get a boy aroused. In this situation some boys might seek sexual relationships elsewhere, but this is not generally true for the girls themselves. They are more interested in love and affection in the present relationship than with sex. This is not to imply that girls are not at all interested in sex; rather, it is a matter of the value priorities in their upbringing.

While it is true that males mature earlier sexually, they reach their highest peak of sexual interest and response at an early age, often before twenty. Gradually and imperceptively this declines, with the sharpest decrease occurring after middle age. Females, on the other hand, starting later and moving forward gradually, continue to increase their sexual activities and response until about thirty years of age. Then they usually stay on a fairly even plateau until well into the fifties or later.

These facts point up the need for more knowledge and information about male and female sexuality for an understanding of heterosexual relationship.

Two specific male sexual processes go on from puberty to advanced old age. The first is the continuous production of sperm together with the accompanying fluids necessary for ejaculation. After puberty, the male is continually sexually potent: he is able to impregnate a woman. The second process is the production of the male sex hormone testosterone which produces and stabilizes the secondary sex characteristics such as hair distribution over the body, the body form and structure, the tone of the voice.

The *specific male sexual response* is traditionally considered to begin at puberty (ages 13 to 15) when the young male is first able to produce sperm and to have an ejaculation. It is certain, however, that the male sexual interest and a kind of sexual response starts much earlier. In this book, we will limit our discussion of male sexual response to sexual arousal that results in the erection of the penis and eventual ejaculation.

Men generally respond rather quickly to physical and psychic stimulation. Their sex instinct is urgent and impulsive. They respond to visual, auditory, and mental sex material, such as the sight of the nude or partially clothed body of a woman, pictures of nudity or sexual activity, sexy jokes, stories or music, conscious or unconscious sexual fantasies, and physical contact with the opposite sex. After boys enter puberty at ages 13 to 14, they may have some regular source of sexual outlet, although the type of sexual behavior changes with growing maturity.

The specific male sexual response is the *erection* of the penis followed by some type of stimulation that leads to the male *orgasm*. The types of male sexual activity that can lead to orgasm are chiefly masturbation, sexual intercourse, dreams, petting or intimate body contact, and homosexual activity. The male may reach orgasm about three minutes or more after stimulation has begun. He is able to control his orgasm within very narrow limits, especially if the stimulation persists.

What is an orgasm in a male? The orgasm is the point of highest sexual pleasure and in the male usually coincides with ejaculation of the semen, though in some cases, ejaculation need not occur. The onset of orgasm is a series of rhythmic contractions of the ejaculation muscle about 4/5 of a second apart. When the phallus or erected penis is being stimulated, especially the crown or tip, by movements of the skin to and fro causing friction, men can identify the onset of orgasm by pleasurable sensations in the testicles, the seminal duct, the inner organs, and the urethra of the phallus. These pleasurable feelings increase little by little until they reach a crescendo during the ejaculation of the semen. The ejaculation which occurs during the male orgasm is a complex process.

Prior to the orgasm, fluid from the seminal vesicles containing the sperm from the testes and the fluid from the prostate gland are mixed by being sprayed against the walls of the urethra. This spraying is caused by the swelling and the rhythmic contraction and expansion of the seminal vesicles and prostate gland and is accompanied by a highly pleasurable sensation, especially when the fluid hits the wall of the urethra. The semen is then collected in the urethra bulb and the ejaculation muscle contacts spasmatically, shooting the sperm through the urethra tube and out the tip of the phallus. A strong muscle closes the opening to the bladder so that urine will not leak out or semen enter.

The events occurring in the sex organs are accompanied by

changes in the rest of the body. Pulse rate, blood pressure, and breathing rate reach a peak. The sex flush, reddening of face and front of the body, is most pronounced. Muscles in many parts of the body begin to tense involuntarily. There is no control over these reactions; they just happen. The muscles of the face tighten and those of the neck, arms, legs, usually contract in spasm. The muscles of the abdomen and buttocks are often contracted. Often the muscles of the hands and feet contract spasmatically. Similar body reactions occur in women.

It is no surprise that a feeling of relief, relaxation, and tiredness follows orgasm. Many young males and a few adult males are able to have successive orgasms (multiple orgasm) with or without ejaculation. But there is usually a *refractory period* during which time the male is unable to repeat ejaculation, and very soon after ejaculation the male loses his erection. This refractory period for some may be a few minutes, for others a few hours or even a day. In other words, the male is definitely limited in the frequency of orgasms in a sex act.

The specific female sexual activities are more complicated than those of the male and have a deeper and more profound effect on her whole life, physical as well as psychic. Specifically, the sex life of the female is dominated by the hormones estrogen and progesterone, which control ovulation. This double hormonal functioning has an effect on personality traits as well as on emotional level.

Because of cultural suppression of women's sexual instinct, women have more difficulty reaching their sexual potential. As James Leslie McCary points out in his book, *Human Sexuality,* "Anthropological investigations have consistently revealed that cultures encouraging women to be completely free in their sexual expression produce women whose amatory reactions are as uninhibited and as vigorous as those of their men. Cultures in which there is approval of women's having orgasms produce women who have orgasms. Cultures withholding such approval produce women who are incapable of orgasm."

Women have a great capacity for orgasm. We are indebted to research in this area especially by Drs. William and Virginia Johnson, and the Kinsey research studies. These studies have dispelled false information that has grown out of folklore about love and sex.

The first sign of sexual response in the woman to sexual stimulation is the moistening of the vagina with lubricating fluid. This first response is not visible, but it does prepare the vagina immediately for the reception of the phallus. The lubrication can occur as a response to kissing, embracing, stimulation in the genital region or of the breasts, or to an erotic train of thought. The next sign of arousal is the erection of the clitoris, an erotic organ in the vulva, which becomes engorged with blood.

Changes occur in the breast during the initial excitement of erotic response. The first of these is the erection of the nipples, increasing in length and diameter as a result of blood vessel engorgement. Later in the excitement phase, the breasts themselves may increase in size as well as the areolas surrounding the nipples.

In the sex organs, the labia (outer and inner) swell and become engorged with blood. These changes are likely to occur quite late in the excitement stage. The vagina also responds to arousal. The outer third reacts differently from the inner two-thirds. As sexual tension mounts, the outer third of the vagina becomes engorged with blood and swells. It is preparing itself to clasp the phallus and also causing the vulva floor surrounding the vagina opening to swell and protrude. This effect also opens the inner and outer lips. The inner two-thirds of the vagina begins to expand and stretch thus causing a ballooning effect. At the same time, the cervix and uterus are pulled up and back, producing a longer and smaller passage. Changes in other parts of the body also may occur at this time: sex flush on the body, heavy and quick breathing, tensing of body muscles, increase in heart beat and blood pressure, sweating. When most of these (or all) have occurred, the woman is ready for intercourse, and orgasm is not far off.

It is normal however, that not every act of intercourse leads to orgasm.

The male should learn about these physical signs and how to bring them about by proper stimulation. While his sexual arousal may be almost instantaneous, he must be aware that a woman generally takes more time to become aroused, especially in the early stages of her sex life. It is important to note that the trust, joy, and affection of a love relationship act as primary sexual stimulators to both persons in sexual intercourse. The person's hand, mouth, body, and sex organs are the physical stimulators. And because such sexual stimulation is expressive of love, it is good and beautiful.

The *female orgasm* is the point of highest sexual pleasure. Little by little the pleasurable sensations mount until they reach a crescendo. The major observable feature of the female orgasm is a series of rhythmic contractions of the outer third of the vagina. A mild orgasm may be three to four contractions, an intense orgasm from eight to twelve. These contractions can be felt by the male as a sort of grabbing sensation on the phallus. At the same time, the neck of the uterus that protrudes into the vaginal canal also contracts rhythmically up and down, often rubbing against the glands of the phallus.

Unlike the male, some females have the capacity to experience multiple orgasms of varying degrees of intensity within a relatively short period of time. This varies from woman to woman. On the other hand, there are other women who seem to experience orgasm infrequently, some not at all.

Some special problems

What has been said in this chapter thus far has come from scientific research. It must be remembered that the physical and psychic aspects of sex vary greatly from person to person. People respond in their own ways to stimulation. This must always be kept in mind in discussing this kind of material. Let us now turn our attention to some problems concerning the sex organs.

Regular *hygiene* is necessary to keep the sex organs free from odors, irritation, inflammation, and infection. Regular bathing will usually suffice. In the male, the glans penis should be cleaned regularly of smegma (a whitish substance) that collects under the foreskin of the uncircumcised. The under clothes should be changed regularly to avoid irritation and infection from urine and other deposits. Wearing clothes which allow the testicles to hang freely is a good practice. In the female, sexual hygiene is likewise a must. The vulva must be cleaned regularly of smegma, urine, and possible fecal deposits. The loose skin around the clitoris should be pulled back and cleaned. Irritation, infection, and inflammation from bacteria are the principal dangers, especially if they get to the internal sex organs. During the menstrual flow, it is important to keep these areas clean and free from bad odors.

Veneral Diseases (VD) are one of the major medical problems of the sex organs. At the present rate of infections, health authorities say, we are headed for a real epidemic. Venereal diseases are highly contagious diseases that affect the sex organs and eventually the rest of the body; they can be caught and passed on by sexual contact.

One of these, *syphilis,* is a highly contagious disease that is transmitted by sexual intercourse or homosexual relations. The germs enters the body at the point of contact: the glands of the penis, the outer and inner labia, vagina, or vagina entrance. Syphilis cannot be caught by touch or by contact with toilet seats. The germ thrives only in warm mucous membranes. The first sign of the disease is a sore (like a cold sore) on the head of the penis, the labia, the vagina, or the vulva. The sore usually appears from a week to a month after infection or contact. After a short time, the sore heals, and the person may think that he or she is cured.

On the contrary, the germ has entered the bloodstream and will begin to attack the body. Some of the effects of VD are heart disease, blindness, paralysis, insanity, and infection of others, including unborn children. Most city health departments now have centers where one can easily be tested for syphilis. A simple blood test, the Wassermann Test (used for persons applying for marriage licenses), is all that is necessary. The cure is usually a series of penicillin shots and other antibiotics. Future contacts with infected people will bring on a recurrence of the disease.

Gonorrhea is another contagious venereal disease that is passed on in the same way syphilis is — through intercourse or homosexual relations. It appears about one to seven days after contact. Rather than entering the body at the point of contact as in syphilis, the germ attacks the mucous membrane of the urethra of the male or the vagina of the female. The first sign of the disease is an itching or burning sensation in the penis or the vagina. This appears especially when the male urinates or the woman has intercourse. In some people, more often in women, the symptoms are hardly noticeable. There is often a discharge of pus from the urethra or the vagina. All these symptoms disappear when the germ enters the body. Only a blood test will confirm its presence. The chief effects of the disease are crippling, sterility, and blindness in unborn children. Again, the cure is penicillin and other antibiotics. Gonorrhea is more common than syphilis and can be caught by further contact with infected persons.

Even though VD is rather easy to cure, it remains a powerful killer today. If left untreated, both forms of the disease can bring painful results, usually ending in death. Since getting infected with the disease means the person has had sexual relations, most people, especially the young, are likely to keep their mouths shut about it. It is this silence born of shame and ignorance that maintains VD as the powerful killer it is.

Among the many other problems relating to sexual relations between male and female, *frigidity, impotence,* and *sterility* rank high. Recent research points up the gravity of the problem today but also indicates that these problems do respond to psychiatric treatment.

Frigidity (in women) refers to disturbances in female sex and sexuality from lack of orgasm and dissatisfaction with sexual stimulation and intercourse. The woman may have no desire for heterosexual relations or even an inability to participate in them.

In this case a woman may not be able to reach orgasm with a man but may reach orgasm through masturbation or lesbian practices. The main cause of frigidity is psychological rather than organic or physiological; it has more to do with her sexuality than her sex. In many cases, the cause can be traced to the overwhelming role of unhealthful conditioning, sexual repression, and premarital experience in erotic response. Such situations can cause frigidity because the focus is too often put on the sex act and not on the person. Spontaneity rather than anxiety is called for; pleasure and sexual response should not be seen as the only goals of sexual intercourse. One can't plan pleasure or response; one can, however, plan a loving relationship.

Scientific finds point up the importance of the husband as loving stimulator and the fact that he must learn the complexity of the woman's body in order to successfully stimulate her sexually. "Sexual stimulation is not a one-way street. The woman should reciprocate with the same sort of fervor that the man extends to her, not only because she wishes to excite and please him, but also because the act of exciting one's lover should be a highly pleasurable and fulfilling experience."

Frigidity is a serious problem, estimated to concern from 33 to 66 percent of women in America. Some recent research indicates that as many as 80 percent derive little or no pleasure from the sex act. The causes of frigidity are numerous, of which the most important seems to be faulty education. More than likely, the frigid woman would have been taught that sex was bad, men were bad, pregnancy was bad, giving was bad. Within the marriage itself, she might resent her husband's relationship to her or his approach to sex. Finally, she might be psychologically unable to relax. Experience shows that in many cases the problem of frigidity responds to professional psychological treatment.

Impotence (in men) is the inability of the penis to achieve erection preparatory to sexual intercourse. As in the case of frigidity in women, impotence is usually a psychological problem though in some cases a disorder in the sex glands may be the direct cause. In such cases, the sex gland disorder may have been caused by some disorder in the nervous system. Ultimately the cause is psychological. Among the major causes are masturbation, homosexuality, poor sex education or view of sex, sexual fatigue by unusual sexual demands by the wife, physical fatigue caused by alcohol or smoking, dread of impotence or sexual inadequacy, which is the need to prove oneself sexually.

Another problem associated with impotence is premature ejaculation, which means the man reaches orgasm before he can insert the phallus or shortly after he does. In some men, ejaculation occurs at the least erotic stimulation. In such cases, a man is unable to satisfy the woman. While a man can control his orgasm within very narrow limits, he does have *some* psychic control over his orgasm. Premature ejeculation is also a psychic problem. As indicated above, impotence reacts favorably to psychiatric help because it is a psychic problem.

Sterility in the male is the inability of the testicles to produce mature sperm; in the female it is the inability of the ovary to produce mature eggs. In either case, impregnation is not possible. Sterility in the male which is caused by absence of sperm or too little sperm to result in conception is difficult to cure. Some success has been had using a hormonal treatment. The problem here is that the present side effects are undesirable: the man begins to take on some of the secondary sex characteristics of the woman. It is to be noted that some writers classify impotence and premature ejaculation under sterility, though it has been explained earlier that these problems are usually psychological and not physical in nature.

Sterility in the female occurs when there is no ovulation, a change in the ovary, a faulty functioning of the ovary, or a defective ovary. In some women sterility may be caused by inflammation or blocked fallopian tubes, a condition which damages or even destroys the fallopian tubes. Other problems may be faulty hormonal functioning and the inability of the uterus to hold its mucous lining, often causing miscarriages.

Because of the number of organs that must function properly in a woman's sexual system, it is no surprise that many women are affected by temporary or permanent sterility. However, new hope has appeared with the results which sterile women are having with the use of synthetic hormones. The problem with this method to date is the inability to control the multiple conceptions that can take place. There are many unanswered questions in this area because no one yet knows exactly how these complex organs work.

Conclusion

Men and women complement and complete each other. The propagation of the human species requires the intimate cooperation of both sexes, not just physically but psychically and spiritually.

Sex is more than the physical union of two bodies; it requires a response from a person's total self, body, mind, and soul. To say that a person can have sex without being affected by it is to shut one's eyes to the reality of human experience. Sex is not a neutral experience. One's sexual values and needs are not like an appendage on the body, separate from the whole; sexual values and needs are an integral part of one's total value system.

If a person says one can have sex any time with anybody and not be affected, that person is reflecting all his or her values, not just sexual values. Many problems that married people have with their spouses and many problems that keep people from getting married lie in the area of male-female sexual differences. The problems begin during adolescent dating and often continue into adult life. An understanding of these differences and responses should go a long way toward reducing frustrations and unhappiness in heterosexual relationships.

Not only must physical sex be integrated with the psychic and spiritual aspects of the person to find is fullest expression, it must also be creative sex if it is to grow and develop. Sexual response, male or female, depends not just on the mechanical use of techniques but on the creative and imaginative use of such techniques. The physical sex organs have a capacity to respond to stimulation as we have described it here, but this response is not automatic. *Nothing can replace a creative, deep, and abiding love of two people for each other as the greatest single source of sexual stimulation.* Max Lerner has stated it well: "If sex is not saying love, joyousness, enchantment, and trust; if sex does not mean serenity, the excitement of exploring the world of the body, the meeting of two personalities in the act of meaningful union — if the new sexual freedom is not saying these things and does not come to say these things, then for all the sense of revolt and liberation it is bringing in its wake, it is not saying much."

11

Sex and Morality

Some say that the United States is probably the most sex-obsessed country in the world. If this is so, then it is not surprising that many people are confused about the meaning, purpose, and function of sex in our society today. There are so many people with so many different ideas about what is right and wrong in sex, it is difficult to determine just whom to listen to. Everyone lives day-to-day with a personal value system that affects concrete decisions; the sexual area is no exception. However, the values others talk or boast about may not necessarily be the values that govern their own decisions in sex. For instance, they may feel they need to put up a front for the gang. For some, morality becomes a bad word because it means a lot of things that they are not supposed to do. "It takes all the fun out of life."

The psychologist Karl Menninger gives a hint to approaching sex morally when he states that not all sex is bad, but there is such a thing as bad sexual behavior. Such behavior is not "bad" because it is "indecent," "orgiastic," etc., *but because it corrupts and destroys the personality of the participants.*

Many adults were brought up more conscious of the bad than the good possibilities inherent in sexual experiences. Maybe they repressed their sexual desires because they were afraid of them; they could see the sufferings around them that came from bad sexual experiences. Maybe they were too occupied with making a living, having children, and fighting wars to work out positive aspects of a meaningful sexual morality. Be that as it may, there is a slowly developing silent revolution in morality, especially sexual morality.

Moralists today say that self-realization of the individual person is the important thing. This attitude is helpful but is negatively reflected in advertisements which appeal directly to the human desire to discover and improve the real self. Use the right product and one will become an irresistible lover, a tiger, a healthy smelling animal, a guy or gal of the "Now" generation.

Duane Mehle in his informative pamphlet, *Sex and the Silent Generation,* says "The secular man of today does not fear the possibility of sin as he fears the possibility of failure . . . Sin is forgivable in the emerging morality since there is no accepted way of measuring right or wrong; but failure is hard to overcome."

One thing adults can learn from the younger generation is how to talk about sex, how to share concern, questions, and doubts. Many adults have believed that sex is really dirty, something to be done in secret and not to be talked about openly. Unconsciously many parents have also passed this idea on to their children. In a big way, the younger generation has helped the rest of us overcome that hurdle. Talking openly about sex, young people want to find out what sex is and where it fits into one's life, where it helps, hurts, how it can serve man in a positive moral way.

Knowing that the body is good and sex is good, they are open to the wonder, beauty, and holiness of sex. "God created man in the image of himself, in the image of God he created him, male and female he created them . . . And so it was. God saw all he had made and indeed it was very good" (Gen 1:26-31). Sex is not only a way to have children, but a revelation of persons through mutual experience. Youth wants to make decisions individually, based on attitude and conduct that helps build genuine respect and create integrity within interpersonal relationships. Sexual morality in the past was mostly a series of do's and don'ts intended to persuade individuals to behave in certain accepted way. Morality was based solely on the acts themselves without regard to motivation. The effect of this morality was limiting individuals in growing into full human beings.

Developing a positive morality

What is morality anyway? Christianity truly lived must involve response. Response, responsibility, and dialogue express the personal relationship *between people*. Specifically, it is God's word calling and inviting people together with the human decision to respond. The content of this response is at the core of morality. Christ's message is addressed to the whole person, to all that is essential in the individual, to the person as a body-spirit totality, to the individual as a unique person and social being. A person is endowed with intelligence, free will, and a power of action whereby he controls his activity. Therefore, a person has a great responsibility, the responsibility of determining one's actions according to the true and the good. Morality then is not law but a free response in love to God calling people to share in his life.

Jaspers says that a person is not something that just "is" but *someone* who decides "what he or she is." By accepting responsibility for one's life, a person finds a place in life, fills it, and thereby fulfills himself or herself. Human responsibility grows out of the concreteness of the person and his situation. An individual goes this way but once; one's destiny will never recur. No one else has one's potentialities nor will anyone else be given them again. Morality then is responsibility for the realization of our potentialities as persons. Certainly the parable of the talents — whether one hides them, uses them, or misuses them — is a challenge to one's capabilities as a human being. At judgment that will be the question asked: What did you do with what I gave you?

Responsibility implies freedom, not just a "freedom from" but a "freedom to" accept responsibility. Being human is being responsible because it is being free. A person is always free to decide on the nature of what one is and what one will become. Viktor Frankl in his book, *The Doctor and the Soul,* states this point well when he says: "Man is not determined by his origins.

His behavior cannot be calculated from the type. Man has the freedom to escape the conditioning factors of types. Man begins to be human only where he has the freedom to oppose bondage to a type. For only there, in freedom, in his very being — being responsible; only there is man authentic."

To be moral means to be free because only when a person is free to decide and to act responsibly can he or she develop to his or her full potential. In all cases one retains the freedom and the possibility of deciding for or against the influence of his surroundings. Some people blame their childhood, parents, education, or environmental influences for making them what they are. They are trying to excuse their own lack of response. This is not to say we are not influenced in some way by these factors. However, every person is responsible to free himself from faults. Each person must reevaluate himself constantly and strive to remove the marks of bad experiences or training. A faulty upbringing exonerates nobody; freedom has certainly to be a conscious effort. It is not an easy task.

Viktor Frankl says: "When man opposes the limitations of nature, when as a human being he takes a stand, when he ceases to be subjugated and blindly adherent to the constraints imposed by the biological factor of race, the sociological factor of class, or psychological factor of characterological type — only then can he be judged morally."

Morality, then has to do with responsibility and freedom, the *right order* of things and what one ought to do as a human being to perfect oneself as a person according to this order. It presents one with an ideal: to reach her or his full potential as a unique human being, to be one's own person. Being created in God's image and likeness is an awesome challenge for each person. It is only in accepting responsibility and freedom that people truly come alive and enjoy life, happiness, and peace. One is free, not a slave to any thing or person. Morality then deals with (a) *human acts* for which a person can be responsible (I accept or refuse), not indifferent acts like eating, sleeping, walking; (b) *free acts,* not acts which man does not control; and (c) acts proceeding does not control; and (c) acts proceeding *directly from the will*, not actions or passions that spring "from nature like the instincts."

The human being is not just an isolated individual in the world but a person who performs acts for which she or he is responsible. This means that the law of the species (the natural order found in reality) or the divine law (the spiritual order found in reality) will not move a person like a pawn at its service. Each person must accept responsibility for these realities, accept or refuse them, re-enact in himself or herself the whole history of humanity.

Therefore, morality deals with intention and human needs. The norm by which a person judges the morality of one's acts is based on the sense of personal integrity and worth which are at the heart of one's interpersonal relations. And loving interpersonal relations are an important need of all human beings. Sexual morality, and all morality, must be judged in this light.

It is necessary to distinguish between the impulses and desires resulting in the arousal of the sex instinct and those acts that proceed from the will. Impulses that proceed from the instinct are of themselves natural and good and therefore cannot be judged morally. Everyone experiences erotic thoughts, desires, and even sexual arousal that results from the first motions of the sex instinct. These are good; they merely prove a man or a woman to be sexually healthy. They are naturally enjoyable; they are part of our humanness.

What is important here is not the first motions of the sex instinct, but what a person consciously does thereafter. What takes over: the power of the instinct or the power of the will? Most important for the individual morally is how he or she develops the sexual function in life. When judging our acts we must ask ourselves: (1) Do they help build genuine respect and create integrity in interpersonal relationships? (2) Do they open communications and enable people to exchange freely and honestly? (3) Do they enable both the individual and the group to survive with joy and satisfaction? *Sex is altruistic,* a matter of a relationship between two persons, and not merely the instinctive physical union of two persons. Altruistic sex doesn't happen; it develops as the person becomes a whole human being. Thus while the first motions of the sex instinct cannot be judged morally, the second motion can.

The purpose of sex in the natural order of reality is the physical union of a man and a woman for procreation in marriage. The purpose of sex in the spiritual order of reality is to foster the mutual love between persons. The possibility of the creation of a new human being is an added spiritual event. Selfishness, sex for pleasure alone, and irresponsible parenthood can only be objective disorder — The objective morality of sex can be judged on these basic ideas. Subjectively, morality is a person's understanding of these ideas, and this is very personal.

The basic question is not how far a person can go but why does one ever begin? Disorder is introduced into sex through selfishness and lack of love. Adolescents should convince themselves of this fact. The real failure in sex is the failure to integrate the sex instinct into the whole person. If a person is really trying to make this integration and to develop his potentialities, he will find fulfillment in his life. A person must judge one's values, attitudes, and practices against these principles:

"Exactly what are my sexual moral values? Do my values enhance my self respect? Do they increase my capacity to trust others? Have I as a human being consented to love and be loved? Is my sex instinct selfish or altruistic? Do my relationships possess a basic honesty?

Adolescent moral questions

One of the basic difficulties in sexual morality is distinguishing basic moral values and principles from sexual customs, practices, and taboos. Over the centuries, Christianity has developed social, religious and moral values and principles in the sexual sphere that reflect the natural and spiritual order of reality. Each succeeding generation adds to the knowledge of the order by its discoveries and insights about the nature of reality — physical, psychological, social, and spiritual. Thus the natural and supernatural order of reality must be thought of as *dynamic,* with each generation having greater knowledge and insight into the values and principles. These are what should be passed on to succeeding generations.

However, each generation tends to safeguard these sexual values and principles by setting up customs, practices, and taboos. The problem develops when a generation tries to pass on the customs, practices, and taboos instead of the values and principles or, what is worse, to pass them off as principles and values. For example: the adult generation may try to enforce as values their dating practices, ideas of modesty, their customs concerning kissing, necking, petting. The younger generation may then reject these customs, practices, and taboos as being outdated, but they may not necessarily be rejecting the values and principles behind the customs.

Every generation must work out its own safeguards. Adults tend to judge the young on what these practices mean to adults and they often do not attempt to find out what they mean to the young. How many times do you hear the statement: "What is this generation coming to?" The real danger to youth is throwing out the values and principles together with the customs, practices, and taboos. *The quality of one's moral life has to be judged against values and principles, not against customs, practices, and taboos.*

The principal source of most adolescent sexual problems comes from the *strength of the sex instinct,* together with confusion about its place among the values of life. Lack of direction and an immature concept of love and sex are not uncommon. Young people need not be discouraged, however; searching and developing in sexual areas are part of adolescent life.

Sexual development follows personality development. The first sexual outlet might be with oneself. The next might be with a friend of the same sex or possibly with someone of the opposite sex. Such patterns are not uncommon with the young adolescent. It has been said that love is the best cure for lust. As one develops an altruistic attitude towards others, one's sex and sexuality will become more and more heterosexual. Another source of difficulty is our culture's pre-occupation with sex; it surrounds a person wherever he goes. Many stores have sex materials readily available to anyone who has the money to buy; the mass media exploit such materials to the utmost. For normal human development it is necessary to integrate the sex instinct into the whole person; to separate sex from the whole person seems to be the aim of our society as seen in the advertising world.

The major sex problems in adolescence find their source not in a lack of control due to human weakness but in a *lack of direction* of the sex instinct. As a hold-over from childhood, basic *selfishness* is still a real part of the life of an adolescent. In sex it usually leads young people to immediate self-satisfaction for the sake of the pleasure involved and for release of sexual tension. Thus masturbation, homosexual practices, heavy necking and petting, and experimentation with sexual intercourse can be judged in some people, not as lack of control, but as pure and simple selfishness. They are using people for their own pleasure, and this is when irresponsible sex is introduced.

He or she is willing, so why not? Failure to solve such problems represents a lack of sexual maturity, an inability to integrate sex into the totality of one's life, and a disregard for the good of others. Failure in this regard has great influence on one's later sex life in marriage. For example, a girl's need for lasting love may lead to meaningless sex. She may find herself in the vicious cycle of seeking love through the medium of sex with one boy after another. Similar things also happen to boys. Such searching can be solved only be experiencing real care, concern, and love from another person. How can one know what love is if one has not experienced it? How does one start looking for love?

Once the sex instinct comes into full play at puberty, the adolescent is faced with moral decision making. Human concern should outweigh *the conflict between values and morals and the strength of the sex instinct*. Often through lack of knowledge the adolescent has difficulty in judging the morality of sex acts. But if the adolescent has been treated humanely, an irresponsible sex act would very probably be seen as an offense against a person, and thus immoral. A boy or girl finds that he or she is readily stimulated by close contact with people of the opposite sex and yet wants to enjoy their companionship and love. Here a negative approach of do's and don'ts is usually ineffective, but a few simple guidelines may help, particularly what is called the principle of double effect.

The principle of double effect begins with the fact that when a person acts, two effects may follow. One effect is desired (good effect) and the other is not (poor effect). Yet both effects, good and poor, follow from the same act. The question is: Should one perform the act? A person may act if the poor effect does not follow from the good effect or if both effects follow simultaneously from the one act, and one does not intend the poor effect in either case. Now applying this principle to sexual actions, one may act if: (a) the first effect is good: one's intention is to develop and foster a friendly relationship and love, and to express this by acts of affection; and (b) the second effect is not intended nor willfully desired: sexual stimulation and sexual arousal. Sexual arousal may result from the act because of the working of the sex instinct, but it was not in one's intention or desire. This points up the principle stated earlier: It is not how far one can go, but why does one ever begin in the first place. It is necessary to get into the habit of being honest with oneself.

Adolescent chastity

What is chastity? Chastity is the purposeful ordering of the sex instinct according to one's state in life. We see from this definition that chastity applies to the married as well as to the single. There are times in marriage when a couple must exercise control: during the honeymoon, before and after the birth of a child, during periods of illness and absence. Chastity has to do with sexual growth.

The *goal of chastity* is order — the control and direction of the sex instinct for a purpose, namely, growth to sexual maturity.

Chastity is sexual maturity; it is the indispensable prerequisite for true love. Sexual control is meaningless without love; so to love implies sexual control. Without direction, the purpose of human sexuality will be defeated and will express itself increasingly in selfish sex. Chastity is a purposeful growing process in sex and sexuality by which one's life is dominated by the love of another and finally the gift of self — a total commitment to another and a total self donation and acceptance. This just doesn't happen; it must be worked at. Selfishness has the head start, but this growing process is the source of sexual morality.

It is possible to give proper direction to the sex instinct if a person uses the *proper means*. Chastity is a continually maturing and expanding process, even into marriage. Some young people make the mistake of relying solely on spiritual means to solve their sex difficulties. When prayer and the sacraments don't seem to work, they give these up altogether as useless. Often loss of faith or religious practice among young people can be traced to unsolved sex problems. A person won't get the spiritual help he needs until he does something in the natural order of things to solve his problem. "Grace builds on nature" — this principle still has meaning.

Some suggested *natural means* will now be considered. General contol of all bodily appetites, passions, and instincts will help a person to direct the sexual instinct. In this regard training of the will is important. If the will operates in all areas of one's life, it will work in sex.

Good physical conditioning through proper exercise and eating habits is important: a sound mind in a sound body. A good body tone will assure good muscle reflex and a healthy nervous system. A rundown body brought on by a pampered life will make more demands on a person than he can meet without harm to himself.

One must also learn how to sublimate his impulses rather than to repress them, for repression tends only to strengthen them. By sublimation a person redirects the energy of the sex instinct creatively into healthy channels. The strength of the sex instinct differs from person to person, and we have suggested here only some of the means one may use. Successful discipline is an individual thing, and there is no surefire method for all. Experience will reveal what works and what doesn't.

Some suggested spiritual means follow. The first and most important is a proper moral attitude and a sense of moral values. If one's attitudes and values are not healthy, then one's attitude toward sex is questionable. On the other hand, if the general direction of a person's moral life is good, then most of the difficulties in sex will not be serious.

Another positive help is the proper understanding of sex, sexuality, and love. This probably has a deeper and more lasting effect than any other single means. Next would be the use of the sources of grace: confession, the Eucharist, and continuing prayer. Throwing oneself on the mercy of Christ in confession, recognizing the fact that people are weak and that they make mistakes and then approaching Christ in the Eucharist to prove one's love can become a powerful help when used with the natural means mentioned above. Finally, prayer will bring one to recognize that before God everyone is in need of redemption, that people really need his help to grow and mature as persons.

Conclusion: Sex and morality

Young people today more than ever before are concerned with the search for role identity. Many see this as a search for fulfilling and meaningful personal relationships, especially with the opposite sex. All this is good, but it has brought in its wake many difficulties and questions. Are young people willing to accept the responsibility of what it means to be involved in the life of someone else? What does it imply? It certainly includes love and some kind of sexual relationship. But to what extent? Does growth in love necessarily require an expression of erotic intimacy or sexual intercourse? These are serious questions that all youth must face and attempt to answer honestly. Every young man or woman so involved has to deal with his or her sex instinct and its consequent stimulation and arousal. In effect, every young person must develop a meaningful set of sexual values that will operate in personal relationships. We are not just referring to the physical and psychological implications but more important, to the moral issues related to the spiritual values and ideals of both parties. It is not just one's own life that is involved but the life of another person.

12

Obstacles to Growth and Maturity

Obstacles to maturity in sex and sexuality are numerous in our culture. Young people are confronted with all kinds of opinions, values, practices, moral opinions, and influences that they often find difficult to judge. Yet every person must choose a path for herself or himself. The greatest danger lies in the far-reaching effect that these influences have on the development of a healthy personality and true growth in sex and sexuality. And most of these values and practices are easy to take because of the soft sell by which they are presented.

Acceptance and respectability are the goal, and economics is often the motive — somebody is probably making money on it. Because most people have a concept of right and wrong, the culture must develop a rationale or logical reasons why they should accept this or that value or practice. There is no end to such rationale in today's communication media.

Some sexual codes found in the culture

It has been mentioned before that Americans have been accused of being overly concerned with sex. Part of this, people say, is the result of our tremendous emphasis on the material aspects of life. Others have pointed to the *Playboy* and *Playgirl* phenomenon which has given the sagging sex ideal a boost of a sort. The crisis of identity in the male and female, they say, is being covered up by these inadequate sex ideals.

This stress on sex and sexuality has brought in its wake new sexual codes, especially noticeable in the removal of old taboos and restrictions and even some sound values. The proponents of the new codes have developed rationales that have gained many followers. In these new codes the concept of sex in and out of marriage takes on new and different meanings. Finally, these new codes try to persuade the young generation to choose new standards concerning pre-marital sex. Let us evaluate each of these new sexual codes and standards.

The first of these new sexual codes is what has come to be called *modern hedonism,* which is the hunger for the sentient, something which will stimulate and give pleasure to the senses. At the basis of this hedonism is the pleasure principle — pleasure for pleasure's sake. American affluence and leisure have opened up the possibility of fun and pleasure for all. Americans can not only afford it; they also have the time for it. The young, in particular, want to taste and experience everything. The slogan of the "now" generation is, "I want it and want it now." The monotony and blandness of American technological life has affected our culture to a degree that it seems that people need a bigger sentient kick to get satisfaction: in hearing — loud and abrupt rhythms in music; in sight — bright and clashing colors; in touch — more intense and passionate ways of making out; in taste — exotic and unusual mixtures in food and drink; in the nervous system — the need for stronger drugs to heighten sensations or relax tensions; in sex — the need for unusual sex acts to gain orgasm.

Hunger for the sentient requires a nervous jolt. Yet the jolt to the nerves causes a more intense hunger, and so the dose must be constantly stepped up for satisfaction. Where will it all end? Whether this represents an escape from bondage, a revolt against the organized system of American culture or a fatalistic attitude toward life is not clear, but that it is a dismaying waste of creativity and of life is clear. Why has it come to this?

Paul Goodman in his book, *Growing Up Absurd,* says: "We

live increasingly in a system in which little direct attention is paid to the object, the function, the program, the task, the need; but immense attention to the role, procedure, prestige, and profit.'' Businessmen through their advertisers are selling modern hedonism to the young because they know youth can afford it.

What does all this mean? The problem seems to center on the spiritual versus the physical in man: man's desire for freedom, responsibility, and meaning versus his desire for fun and pleasure arising from the demands of his senses, appetites, passions, and instincts. Viktor Frankl in his book, *Man's Search for Meaning,* states that the pursuit of happiness is self-defeating. The more a person directly seeks fun and pleasure, the more it eludes him.

Happiness, peace, fulfillment, and meaning are by-products. They are side-effects of a reason to be happy, to be at peace, to be fulfilled, to have meaning — a person to love, a cause to be committed to, a God to serve.

In any case, we are inclined to overestimate the positive and negative aspects of pleasure or of the pleasant or unpleasant tone of our experiences. Frankl states that the underlying motivation of all human behavior is not Freud's will-to-pleasure but what he calls man's will-to-meaning. Pleasure is incapable of giving meaning to life. Of itself pleasure is not the goal of our aspirations but the consequence of attaining them. Has contemporary man become weary of the spiritual? Freedom and responsibility belong to the spirit of man. Today it appears important to remind man that he is spiritual, not just physical.

Another moral code is what has come to be called the *playboy or playgirl ideal,* which proposes to use sex as recreation. At a time when the male and female role in society is being seriously questioned, it is no accident that the magazines *Playboy* and *Playgirl* sell millions of copies. The publishers have stepped into the vacuum to give the American male and female a normative identity image. Combining sex with culture, they have created sophisticated magazines that can be displayed and bought openly on the public market. They possess a philosophy and an attitude toward life, sex, and morals, and by mixing truth with half-truth, they try to impress the public by providing facile solutions to complex problems and unjust laws or situations.

The cardinal principle of the playboy or playgirl approach to sex is a casualness whereby a person doesn't become attached to anything or anybody. "Live life to the hilt" is its motto, interpreted as a basic selfishness which sees people as nothing more than things to be used. The playboy or playgirl is one who has a sort of urbane earthiness and sophistication inspired by self-centeredness.

The *playmate* is the symbol of recreational sex. Sex is entertainment, not commitment — a leisure activity that can be flicked on and off like a commercial. When playtime is over, the function of the playmate ceases. The person becomes an object, a packageable item in a consumers' market. Hugh Hefner, whose Bunny Clubs have been called a Disneyland for adults, looks upon himself as the greatest apostle of the American sexual revolution and the father of modern hedonism. He lampoons puritanism, censorship, overbearing religious organizations, and anti-sex laws. He hits all the things that people are generally against. He favors the American dream of freedom, creativity, and individuality. He favors all the things people are for. How can he fail?

These magazines sell anti-sex and unreality instead of the real thing. However nice and desirable, the playmate just isn't like the boy or girl next door. A real person isn't that playmate in the centerfold, a departmentalized item, a commodity that can be turned on and off. Sex is not an accessory of life; it is an integral part of life. In the recreational concept of sex, people become objects to be manipulated, thus completely depersonalizing sex. This viewpoint will surely fail to mature a person in one's total personality. Such a person will remain adolescent, ambivalent, and indecisive about sex.

Some may object that they don't see all this in *Playboy* or *Playgirl*. If they did, they probably wouldn't buy them — or read them. They may argue that the magazine has fine articles — it has.

But it could be asked, are teenagers reading those fine articles? It is unfortunate that the publishers are selling a kind of sex to the young that is far removed from the realities of life. Ultimately, this kind of sex is doomed to failure as fun because it isn't really human. In our evaluation, the main criticism is not directed to some of the fine features found in the magazines but to the philosophy that they are trying to sell.

Since *Playboy* and *Playgirl* were such financial successes, other magazines and newspapers have appeared on the scene. In contrast, they depict aspects of sexuality that offend human taste and sensibility. Such misinformation about sexuality makes it difficult to help people approach sex in a positive and healthy way.

American youth are reflecting the ideal of the *person-centered morality* by removing cultural and religious taboos and restrictions, and by substituting an openness and freedom in sex. The person-centered approach to sex and sexuality considers the sexual drive from the point of view of the individual. It appraises the use or misuse of sex on whether it helps or hurts the person in his or her development. The difficulty with this approach is that it focuses too much on what leads to the perfection of the individual rather than of society. Modern hedonism and the playboy and playgirl ideals are examples of this difficulty.

While in the past Christianity determined and legislated for the community, the person-center morality of our secular culture is determined and self-legislated through individual decision and experience. This has come to be known as *situation ethics* — the person in the concrete situation, not some objective law, decides what is moral.

According to this view, morality deals with human relations, not absolute laws. Situation ethics puts people at the center of concern, not things or laws. The legalist asks, "What does the law say?" The situationist asks, "Who is to be helped." In situation ethics the Christian is commanded to love people, not principles, objects, or any other thing. No values possess inherent good. For too many people, however, these views are translated into a kind of morality of the moment: "I'm right, I'm not hurting anybody; therefore I'll do it."

Many young people look at the phoniness of adult society with its double standard of morality, its sexual hangups, and its inability to talk openly and meaningfully about sex, and they reject this as meaningless for their own lives. They see a father who goes to a topless restaurant while attending a convention but yet refuses to talk with his son about the problems of voyeurism. Again, he may like to see girls and young women in miniskirts and bikinis, but refuses to let his daughter wear them.

As a result, some young people have been caught up in a revolution and have adopted the person-centered morality. They feel that every person must determine the nature and depth of relationships she or he wants with members of the opposite sex. These young people want to make decisions individually, and they believe the path to morality is through self-discovery.

Some of the characteristics of the new morality among youth are frank communication, individualism, and a private system of morality. Its outward expressions are seen in such things as mini or maxi skirts, early dating practices, open talk on sex, room visiting privileges in college, unmarried young men and women living together in what are deemed by them to be meaningful relationships.

Sexually the emphasis is on openness and an experimental approach to love and sex. They want to get at the core of love and sex by trying it out. They form relationships, including sexual ones to see if they work. They know that the *vital element of love or mutual relationship must accompany sexual experience, and that this alone justifies it.* This openness in sex and love can lead, however, to the attitude that one can do as he pleases as long as it doesn't hurt anybody. And the stress on "individual" decision-making sometimes leads to the attitude that "I" should not be concerned with what the other person decides.

Many problems result from the adoption of the ideas of situation morality when it rejects moral absolutes in themselves. It does not take into consideration that the so-called absolutes are not static values and principles but a dynamic view of reality that humanity has been developing over its entire history. These absolutes do not change so much as human understanding of them as people discover more about the human-divine reality. In this sense we can think of the moral values and principles as future absolutes that will find their full realization in humanity's ultimate union with God.

In the sexual areas, the reasons for the person-centered approach are often more romantic than real. For example, if one decides to reject completely the Christian view of the totality of the person, he or she might begin to pretend that sex is a purely biological function. This necessarily would endanger its value and meaning in one's life. No one gets more out of sex than one brings to it.

The Christian sees sex quite differently from many people in the modern secular society. Christianity presupposes a God who created people to enjoy certain forms of communication and relationships. It presupposes that God has a specific intention for the gift of human sex and sexuality. It offers a standard by which sexual relationships might be *measured,* a judgment by which sexual relationships might be redeemed. And in Christianity, sex is connected with procreation as well as love.

Christianity compares sexual union in marriage to the union existing between Christ and his Church. Perhaps sex is ultimately a symbol of the love with which God loves people. Successful sexual relationship involves more than the simple satisfaction of self. It is the self-surrender of two people to each other to form a single identity. While sex implies procreation, it also implies that the man and woman also fulfill each other through a loving, sexual relationship. Sex, therefore, is both the symbol and the substance of a larger union of body and spirit which a woman and a man, through God's grace, may experience together. This is the moral value that Christianity puts on sex.

One of the most persistent sexual codes advanced today is *pre-marital sex.* By pre-marital sex we are talking about sexual intercourse and all that it implies between two unmarried persons. The Sex Information and Education Council of the United States in its publication, *Pre-marital Sexual Standards,* lists four major standards operating today in our culture: "(1) *Abstinence:* the formal standard forbidding intercourse to both sexes; (2) *Double Standard:* The Western World's oldest standard, which allows males to have greater access to coitus than females; (3) *Permissiveness with Affection:* Attitudes favoring this standard have grown in popularity — intercourse is accepted for both sexes when a stable affectionate relationship is present; and (4) *Permissiveness without Affection:* Coitus is accepted for both sexes on a voluntary basis regardless of affection. This last standard has a quite small number of followers, but it is most newsworthy and thereby misleads the public as to the size of the following."

The problem of love and how to recognize it in one's life are basic questions in most of these standards. This love seems to mean a sort of subjective feeling of deep affection based upon a more than casual acquaintance with the other person. The number of adherents to these four standards is hard to determine, but recent studies have indicated a sharp shift of attitudes since the 1920's.

The number of people who advocate abstinence has not changed much since Kinsey made his study in the 1940's and is still the dominant code for most women and a sizable number of men, especially under age twenty. The double standard has lost many adherents, especially among the young. Permissiveness with affection has grown in acceptance and respectability among both sexes at the expense of the double standard and permissiveness without affection. It would seem that that biggest change in the pre-marital sexual code among the young is the idea of a legitimate choice of standards among valid alternatives. Even those who accept abstinence give others the right to choose among the standards. Let us now take a look at those four standards.

It would seem that the *double standard* and *permissiveness without affection* could be classified under the heading of *sex for pleasure.* The adherents to these two standards hold the idea that sex and the pleasure derived from it are of themselves legitimate ends of sex and not just a means to something deeper such as an expression of love. The philosophy here is someone to love and another to use; try before you buy; test it out, see if it works. For males, it is the view that "This is my girl friend and I think so much of her that I wouldn't touch her sexually. I want her to be a virgin when I marry her. Yet I think nothing of laying another girl who is willing. I get my sexual kicks on the side."

Some say that the male needs sexual experience before he marries so he can teach his wife. "Try it out for experience." Sexual intercourse before marriage is no preparation for marriage because in reality it tests little. In particular, it is hardly calculated to keep love creative, let alone alive and growing. It creates an artificial state and isolates sexual experience from the total pattern of their values and their lives together.

This is not an uncommon attitude among some young people today, a hold-over of the double standard of the previous generation. At the basis of such an attitude is a selfishness and a misdirected sex instinct that says it's all right for the man but not for the woman. Such a person often finds it difficult to achieve sexual harmony later in marriage. Then as now, there will be one to love and another to use.

Superficial sex flees the obligation of love becuase such ties involve responsibility. A person must face the consequences of having sex with someone he or she loves. Otherwise, all one can say is, "I had this one and what I've had I can swap, and what I possess I can change. In this kind of sex, I can go after the *type* instead of a particular person." The *type* depersonalizes and collectivizes people so that what is important is not the quality of the satisfaction and happiness but the quantity of sexual pleasure. The *type* cannot burden one with responsibility — if one is careful. Being impersonal, he or she is easily replaceable, and one has no obligation. One can "get love" but need not love. The person is more like property without personal traits or value of her or his own, so there is no question of faithfulness. Such people restrict themselves merely to sex for pleasure. They do not expect to experience love; everything is sex. Such people who are so casual about their sexual experiences use sex as an outlet, as a person might use an alcoholic release for sexual tensions. Quantity of sexual pleasure and instinctual gratification take the place of quality. The supposition is that the experience will some day lead to sexual compatibility and sexual harmony, but it rarely does. Terman at the University of Stanford has shown that the more promiscuous a person is before marriage, the less likely it is that he or she will be maritally happy and achieve sexual harmony.

In superficial sex the accent is shifted from the psychic and spiritual qualities of sex to purely physical gratification. Suddenly the sex instinct demands as much gratification as possible. In getting satisfaction the person departs more from the psychic-spiritual aspects and becomes less capable of mastering the synthesis and integration of sex with his higher powers. The multiplication of disappointing experiences drives the person down the lower plane of mere physical sex, never daring to attempt a truly fulfilling love life. When we set pleasure as the whole meaning of sex, we guarantee that life shall inevitably seem meaningless. Often prostitution is as much a psychological problem for the client as for the prostitute or for anyone who has intercourse outside a love relationship. It nurtures the attitude toward sex for both parties which takes sex as selfish, a mere means to the end of pleasure, pure sensualism.

Why shouldn't someone take it if the other is willing or one is going to pay for it? The fact of the matter is that those who use sex as release are not refreshed by sex. A study made at the University of Wisconsin showed that the girls on campus who engaged freely in pre-marital sex on a regular basis (with or without love) all suffered some psychological problem that required a psychiatrist. It could well be that some of them had earlier psychological difficulties which they tried to remedy by free sex. In any case, the use of sex for release did not achieve its purpose, nor does it make for growth in personality; for a person gets no more out of sex than he brings to it.

Sex to release tension or for pleasure also encourages neither the sexual freedom a person will need in marriage not the pursuit of the many values needed for maturity. How can one expect to shift from a sex-just-for-fun attitude in dating to a sex-as-a-means-of-expressing-love attitude in marriage? The particular habits of physiological and emotional response which now regulate sexual response cannot be transformed overnight or harmonized with the psychical and spiritual expectations of response to one's partner in love. People don't walk up the aisle with one idea of sex and come down the aisle with another. The marriage ceremony of itself does not change attitudes and values toward sex. Sex for release, by its nature, enslaves the rest of a person's potential creativity unless it is harmonized with the total pattern of one's life.

Sex which should be the means of expressing love is made subservient to pleasure and the gratification of the instincts. Sex pleasure becoming an end in itself reduces sex to mere animal instinctual gratification and debases the partner to the level of a mere instinctual object. These attitudes and practices are likely to block the way to the right kind of love life in which sex is the crowning glory of love, the physical expression of the psychic-spiritual union.

Further, sex for pleasure alone does not foster a monogamous attitude or one of trust and faithfulness. The unity and community of persons cannot be achieved in the pelvic region, no matter what techniques and accessories are used. To develop the ability to choose a right partner, young persons must acquire a degree of sexual insight which leads to the integration of the physical aspects of sex with the rest of the personality. To develop the ability and desire to be faithful, they must try to grow beyond the mere physical and instinctual attraction to what the person is.

They should begin to realize how relatively unimportant outward attractiveness is and how much more important are the psychic and spiritual qualities of the person. Stress on appearance leads to a general overestimation of the value of beauty in sex life. The person as such is devalued and the qualities of mind and spirit are overlooked. Marriage increases the opportunity for sexual experience which expresses mutual needs and aspirations, and which can offer revelation, but this opportunity is lost to people blinded to anything but the physical quality of their sex partners.

The sexual code of most people is *abstinence*. We may often hear, "Everybody's doing it, so why shouldn't I?" According to studies at the Kinsey Institute at the University of Indiana, 35 percent of men and 55 percent of women had no pre-marital sexual experience before marriage. The fact is that the choice of a pre-marital sexual standard is a personal moral choice, and many people choose to reserve sexual intercourse for marriage.

Those who advocate abstinence feel that sex and sexuality are not isolated aspects of the self. They are a basic reflection of the total value system, of the type of person one really is. Two persons are not ready for love, sex, or marriage who are not psychically and spiritually prepared to weave new patterns, find new meanings and create common values together. For many, abstinence remains a matter of morality.

Sex cannot be isolated from the rest of life; sexual values cannot be isolated from the total value system which operates in a person's life. Sex needs love, and sex and love need marriage and a home to challenge, preserve, and increase the creative power of sex and love in the lives of two persons. The Catholic Church is very explicit on this position: Sexual intercourse is to be reserved for marriage. To date no adequate substitute has been found in which sex and love can be fused as creatively as in the vocation of marriage. Creation of a home brings sex and love to fulfillment because it unites persons in creative intercourse in every dimension of their lives, not just the sexual. In this atmosphere the quality of their sexual experience will be kept alive and growing because here sex is not just a moment of temporary gratification in a psychic or spiritual vacuum but is found in the totality of two beings in love. The marriage and the home protect against the difficulties in a sexual relationship because there are many other areas in a life together that can satisfy two partners.

The final standard we will discuss is probably the fastest

growing one today, *permissiveness with affection*. In the past few years there has sprung up the practice of two people playing at love, sex, and marriage. These relationships are not identified with promiscuity because there is a meaningful love between the two persons. This practice is probably an outcome of the long dating period that now exists in our culture and the natural consequence of steady dating. It is the next step in the dating game, a meaningful relationship. This practice could also be the natural result of the new freedom among the young at home and in society. The phenomenon of young people going off on their own and living in their own apartments undoubtedly is also a factor.

The questions being asked today are vital. Do sex and love need marriage? If a boy and girl really love each other and agree to sex, why is it wrong? If they really protect themselves against venereal disease and pregnancy, if they don't take themselves too seriously, and decide to express their love for each other in sexual intercourse until their mutual attraction ceases, what harm do they do? If two people can symbolize the unity they feel and celebrate their joy and commitment to each other by sexual intercourse, why should they wait for marriage? What does a marriage ceremony add to love and sex anyway? These are hard questions that need serious consideration.

Such questions indicate that the persons who engage in meaningful relationships know that love and sex are more than physical thrills. In spite of this, experience indicates that the outside marriage sex tends to be more damaging than rewarding. While one may hear of many successful exploits and adventures, pastors, counselors, and psychiatrists paint another picture, one of unwanted pregnancies, of broken hearts and lives stemming from broken commitments to eternal love, of young men and women who have been adversely affected by such relationships.

The prevailing attitude of most young people today is not a rejection of all moral standards, but an honest search for those that are higher and more meaningful — and therefore more permanent — than the old ones based on fear.

We return to the words of Genesis when Adam said of Eve, "This at last is bone of my bone and flesh of my flesh." There is a mysterious unity that takes place during the act of sexual intercourse. No one knows or can predict what effect such a union or sexual experience, with or without love, will have on the immature and developing psyche. There is no sexual relationship, however, without irrevocably meshing and affecting the non-physical selves of the two people involved.

The question a person must honestly ask himself: "Am I willing to invest a portion of my total self and also involve another person, without the sureness of knowing what this sexual involvement will produce?" The risk of hurting each other is great, for there is no reason to expect a continuing experience of meaning in love and sex separated from the totality of a couple's lives together. Sex is never neutral — it will have an effect one way or another.

Persons may think that they can find togetherness through sex, but in fact sex becomes rather routine when the two forget that sex is most meaningful to them when they feel close to each other in many other ways. Confidence, empathy, openness, understanding, and trust have to be established before any meaningful sexual experience can take place. If sexual relations are begun before a couple have found deep friendship, there will be little chance of finding it afterward. If sexual relations do not signify the art of growing, totally and together, how will this growing be expressed in the future?

"Am I honest? What is my aim in seeking sexual enjoyment detached from total commitment and total self-donation? Am I rationalizing by saying that I am not hurting my partner? Is he or she mature enough to say yes, conscious of the effects? Can we both walk away from the relationship assured that we have not hurt each other and have actually grown from our relationship together? Does my attitude really amount to a demand upon my partner for sexual gratification free of other values and claims, explicit or implicit? Is what I am doing really moral?"

These are the questions that must be honestly answered by the advocates of permissiveness with affection in a meaningful relationship.

When sex is an experience that two people have in the midst of other joys and sorrows, it contributes to the ongoing understanding and trust of both, and it develops a quality not otherwise attainable. Love and sex must be put to work in a life together; only then do they become creative. Sexual experience needs every emotional and circumstantial encouragement it can get if it is to be a growing experience of enrichment, kept at its highest peak of quality.

The main question to be answered is: Can two people find outside of marriage any pattern of living that will give better support to the meaning and intent of their love for themselves and others? Experience suggests that love and sex cannot stay alive without developing something more in the lives of the partners. In sexual experiences, two persons can endure frustrations, intensified by love itself, if there exists a richer pattern of life together fostered by this love. Sex needs the continuing mutual commitment of both persons demonstrated in every possible way.

For the Christian, we must say that the sexual act is constitutive; it consummates. When a man and a woman take part in sexual intercourse, they communicate a part of themselves to each other and produce, for a moment, a unity and a culmination. It is God's intention that this unity be perpetuated within the marriage bonds. Christ's help, given through the grace of the sacrament, intensifies this personal union. For the committed Christian there can be no reason for casual or recreational sex outside of marriage. Those who wait to consummate their love after the sacrament of marriage have answered to each other and to the community the questions implied by marriage.

"Yes, we do care enough for each other to promise before all men and God to accept full responsibility for growing in love and sex. Yes, we feel sure enough of our love to pledge ourselves publicly to each other as members of a larger community of man that makes our values possible."

Thus the marriage bond, publicly pronounced in a ceremony,

is a public commitment through a symbolic act. It testifies to the solidarity of love between the two persons and the relation of that love to the community. The marriage itself is *the* sign (the only public sign), that the couple has by which to show the total commitment of each one to the other.

Many young men and women today have become skeptical of the need for marriage because they have seen many marriages which had no meaning. "The marriage ceremony," they say, "signifies nothing; it is only the actual relationship that matters." Although we can't blame sensitive men and women for being frequently scandalized by the institution of marriage, we can't agree with any de-emphasis of the importance of the sacrament and ceremony of marriage.

If a couple truly give their lives to each other in a total commitment, what the marriage ceremony does is actually to establish this to the community. It is *the* affirmation that the couple wants to say openly, "Yes, we know what the sacrament of marriage demands, but are confident that its grace will make it work for us." Any couple who believe that they are living together with a true commitment to each other but who are unwilling to marry must seriously ask themselves why. If they criticize marriage, what they are criticizing is simply the public testimony to the fact that they now live with a mutual promise of deep love and commitment.

There can be no denying that the choice of a premarital sexual standard is ultimately a personal moral choice. In this sense the individual is free. In fact, the choice will depend upon one's value system, especially in the sexual area. While free to choose, the Catholic cannot ignore the traditional teaching of the Church concerning pre-marital sex. Because of its purpose, as explained here, sexual intercourse is restricted to marriage.

In this section we have considered four sexual codes in contemporary life: *modern hedonism,* the *playboy/playgirl ideal,* the *person-centered morality,* and *premarital sex.* Each of these codes in one way or another presents some kind of obstacle to growth and maturity in love, sex, and sexuality. These codes, individually or collectively, leave much to be desired when we consider the tremendous possibilities of human love, sex, and sexuality. If anything, they over-emphasize the individual, physical qualities of sex, ignoring the deeper and more satisfying psychic, relational, and spiritual qualities. Sex must be integrated with the total personality of each partner if it is to avoid the hang-ups fostered by these four codes.

Sexual aberrations inhibiting sexual maturity

Obstacles to growth and maturity in sex and sexuality are known as *sexual aberrations,* the use of sex for a purpose for which it was not intended. In general, such disorders are selfish sex as opposed to altruistic sex. In particular, they include such practices as masturbation and homosexuality.

Selfish sex shows itself in sex for fun or pleasure alone. The problem of selfish sex is more acute in men than in women. Women tend to realize the goal of sex-in-love because they more often feel sexual desire only when the physical longing is conjoined to a desire for psycho-spiritual union. Men, whose sexual urges are more insistent and whose desire for immediate pleasure is more acute, do not gain this attitude without a struggle. A woman tends to give a man what he is looking for, and the man once satisfied never gives the woman more. She may become responsive to a man's desire and give him what he needs and wants, but she too wants to be taken seriously for what she is, a loving human partner who also needs satisfaction.

If love and sex in a person are ever to become altruistic, they must make a shift from self-absorption, from using others, to entering into patient concern for the other partner. Fortunately, casualness about sex is not as strong as every person's desire to be cared for and to care. People can't set themselves up as vending machines that dispense refreshment or consolation. To treat another as an instrument of amusement is to be selfish, and the result can only be lonely isolation — a sort of dying. Being human is being alive and creative as a person; one's sex and sexuality cannot be isolated from this aliveness and creativity.

Another sexual aberration which has its basis in selfishness is masturbation, sex turned in on the self. Masturbation, either male or female, is sexual self-stimulation leading to orgasm. In the male this would include ejaculation of semen. It is usually practiced in solitude, but it may also occur in the company of another person of the same or opposite sex. In this case it is called mutual masturbation.

Its occurrence in early adolescence indicates that masturbation is part of puberty. However, some people persist in this practice into late adolescence and early adulthood, even into marriage. Initially it does disappear when a person first falls in love, but then it may return. Formerly its persistence was considered a sign of sexual immaturity, an arrested sexual development.

Why is there a persistence of masturbation for some into later adolescent years and early adult life? Part of the answer might be the longer period that young men and women remain in dependent roles. Modern culture has effectively lengthened adolescence. Although the young are better informed and more independent than before, their emotional development is still in its early stages. Another reason may be found in dating practices. Today's young people are in the dating stage from ages thirteen to twenty-three. If they are dating week after week, perhaps making out without engaging in intercourse, boys especially may seek relief from the build-up of sexual tension by masturbating. The psychological effect of masturbation on sexual growth and sexual maturity is not fully determined, but it is doubtful that it is healthful. The morality of the act also should be judged as the person grows and matures into adulthood. Sex turned in on self is selfishness, and this is a moral question.

What are some of the *causes of masturbation?* There are not real physical causes; the causes are basically psychological. The *normal psychological cause* of masturbation is curiosity due to self-stimulation and the discovery that the body is pleasurable, as are the sensations it produces. These early experiences often lay the basis for future acceptance of sex as desirable and pleasurable. And for some, early masturbation may represent a struggle to achieve a sense of identity and a sexual self-image. As mentioned above, both males and females masturbate to release sexual tension that has built up. It is natural for masturbation to be accompanied by sexual fantasies.

There are also *abnormal psychological causes* for masturbation, especially if it is habitual or it persists into adult life. Among these are boredom, frustrations, loneliness, poor self-image, inadequate heterosexual relationship, conflict with parents, pressures in school. If the cause is natural, the problem will usually pass with maturity, but if the cause is abnormal, that is, due to some cause other than sex, the problem will be eliminated only when the initial cause is removed. Masturbation can be a sign of a disturbed development or a misguided attitude toward love and life. If a person suffers from sexual frustration, this indicates his or her sex instinct is not yet subordinated to or integrated with the psychic and spiritual powers. But it is not to be inferred that masturbation in every case is a growth or psychological problem. Sometimes it can be a serious moral problem. In this case, a person should seek spiritual guidance. Many young people are worried about the *effects of masturbation*. They have heard all kinds of stories of what would happen to them if they continued to masturbate. According to the Sex Information Center in the United States, "Medical opinion is generally agreed today that masturbation, no matter how frequently it is practiced, produces none of the harmful effects about which physicians warned in the past. The physical effects of masturbation are not significantly different from the physical effects of any other sexual activity."

The harmful effects of masturbation are usually psychological or spiritual. Many young boys or girls have suffered mental turmoil because of guilt about masturbation. And this turmoil often helps cause the practice to become compulsive. For some this results in psychological problems because they seem to have no control over a practice which is considered immoral.

Of itself masturbation cannot cause insanity or psychological damage, but the feeling they have done something wrong, committed sin, and knowing they can't stop leaves some adolescents with a feeling of helplessness. These feelings may also occur when young people are overwhelmed by the experience of orgasm, especially if they are not prepared for it. Parents and counselors can be of great help in offering understanding and gentle advice.

Another effect is that continued masturbation past puberty may turn the individual in on himself and herself. The sexual attitude of the person may remain infantile and become a source of problems in loving. In fact, he or she is only physically active in sex, but not psychically or spiritually. The sex act lacks any object outside of self or any directedness toward a partner. Basically, masturbation is in itself a form of selfish sex, and, as such, it must be considered in its relation to morality.

Masturbation is morally wrong because it is an immature use of sex for a person's own pleasure, because it is an act which turns a person in on himself and thus fails to prepare him for the gift of himself to another in marriage. However, to say that masturbation is morally wrong is *not* to say that every act of masturbation is a mortal sin. Many such acts are slightly sinful, some not at all, especially for young persons who are struggling with their growing up process.

Even though the sex instinct is strong at puberty, young people can work effectively against this type of sexual expression by seemingly indirect means. They need to try to be more and more concerned with other people and about the ways they can be helpful to them. Doing this, they will become less self-centered, giving less attention to their own convenience and thus developing the wholeness of personality necessary for the giving of self to another in love. It is well known that the best cure for lust is love because the energy of the sex instinct is channeled and satisfied. Meanwhile, this concern for others may help to reduce the anxiety a person feels about masturbation, and this lessening of worry may in itself weaken the habit.

We have previously described the natural and spiritual means that a person can use concerning chastity. These can become a source of strength, an aid to getting through difficult moments in the struggle. Finally, it will be of great help to have the advice of a competent person, particularly one who loves and understands young people.

Sexual abberration can also take the form of *homosexuality* and *lesbianism,* that is, sex acts directed to persons of the same sex. Technically speaking, homosexuality refers to sexual acts between males, and lesbianism refers to sexual acts between females. To avoid confusion, however, we will use the general term homosexuality to include lesbianism.

The physical or psychological homosexual is not a modern phenomenom, but today there is increasing concern about this ever growing problem. Homosexuals themselves are fighting legally and socially for acceptance. A new openness and acceptance in certain quarters of society, especially in the fashion industry, in the arts, and in other social areas have prompted many books and magazine articles on the subject.

For most people, the question is not so much one of understanding as one of acceptance of the fact. They can understand, or try to, the physical, psychological, and spiritual problem but have difficulty accepting the demands of the homosexual, especially if these demands include public acts of affection, love, and marriage. Most people feel that public decency and the common good also have rights that must be considered. The modern problem of homosexuality also concerns those non-homosexuals who take up the practice as a variation of their heterosexual activities. Their number seems to be growing.

According to the Sex Information and Educational Council of the United States Study Guide entitled *Homosexuality,* homosexual behavior refers to "overt sexual relations, or emotional attachments involving sexual attraction, between individuals — male or female — of the same sex . . . . Homosexuality and heterosexuality are not discrete entities. Sexual arousal by a member of one's own sex is not an all-or-none phenomenon but a matter of degree . . . ''

Thus homosexuality is a way of thinking as well as a way of acting. Further, the performance of homosexual acts is not, in itself, evidence of homosexuality. While the above definition covers a wide range of people, most people today use the term to apply only to individuals who more or less feel an urgent sexual desire toward and a sexual responsiveness to members of their own sex and who seek to have sexual acts predominantly in this way. In other words, they are practicing homosexuals. There might also be present an aversion to sexual relations, but not necessarily social relations, with the opposite sex.

The prevalence of homosexual behavior has not been fully determined, but it is estimated that approximately 37 percent of all males have engaged in one or more overt homosexual acts at one or more times in their lives. For females the incidence is approximately half that for males. This does not mean that 37 percent of the male population is homosexual. Many boys at puberty pass from the auto-sexual stage of masturbation to the nearest sexual outlet, a close friend with whom he may have one or more sexual acts. This does not make a boy an exclusive homosexual. Homosexuality, as we have defined it, does not really appear fully developed until the post-adolescent period. Of the 37 percent, it is estimated that 4 percent of all white males are exclusive and practicing homosexuals. This is a still large number, and there may be potential homosexuals who never commit an overt homosexual act.

Can homosexuals be identified? Contrary to common belief and the practice of labeling the effeminate male as a homosexual, there are no physical signs of homosexuality. It is interesting to note that females with male characteristics do not tend to be considered in the same way. Because homosexuality is not a disease but a sympton of a personality disorder, it can affect any type of male or female. Studies have shown that only about 15 percent of effeminate males are actually practicing homosexuals. The percentage is 5 percent for female "tom-boys." In fact, many of the so-called male gay bars and homosexual clubs are set up to attract strong male types. On the other hand, because effeminate men tend to join the art professions of theater, design, and clothing, they get more publicity if they are homosexuals. Similarly, some of the tough motorcycle club members in some parts of the country are known homosexuals. Evidence has indicated also that there is also some homosexuality among professional football players. The point we are making here is that homosexuals, male or female, cannot be identified by any specific physical characteristic; it is a psychological, not a physical, problem.

What are the causes of homosexuality? It is agreed to date there is no physical evidence of homosexuality as a disease. A man or a woman from birth does not possess any instinctive desire to have sex only with someone of the same sex. As we mentioned earlier, the sex instinct needs to be ordered and directed by the person. Sexual behavior is at any given time the result of learning and experience the person has had. Therefore, homosexuality is a symptom of a personality disorder; its cause is psychological. It is a *misdirected* sex instinct. By saying the cause is psychological, we are not saying homosexuals are mentally ill or neurotic, though they may be so as the result of strain and conflict. To date, the cause of homosexuality has been determined from evidence given by homosexuals who have sought psychiatric treatment. Whether these causes apply to all homosexuals is not certain. Medical science has not defined the full implications of homosexuality.

The factors that seem to play a key role in causing homosexuality are: inappropriate identification with the opposite-sexed parent, an overpossessive mother for a boy or an overpossessive father for a girl, fear or hostility toward either parent, reversal of masculine-feminine roles in parents, a strong mother and a Milquetoast father, or vice-versa, cultural overemphasis on stereotypes of the male or female which produces feelings of inadequacies to fulfill expectations, a rigid dichotomy of male-female social roles and consequent feelings of not being able to fit these roles, easy access to physical intimacy with someone of the same sex in adolescence which becomes a habit, homosexual seduction of a child by an adult. It is evident from this list of causes that the tendency toward homosexuality begins early in a child's life and is usually centered in the home, but it does not often reveal itself fully until early adult life, somewhere in the twenties.

Can homosexuality be cured? Because of the uncertainty of its specific causes, homosexuality is hard to cure. Some people have actually been changed from exclusive homosexuals to exclusive heterosexuals, but they are few in number. Much more success has been attained in helping the homosexual to limit his overt sexual behavior. Some success has also been achieved in helping the homosexual to enjoy both homosexual and heterosexual acts. Much more has to be studied in this area, especially in determining causes. What is implied here is the need to know more about human sexuality.

More important to society are the *preventive efforts* that need to be used to make sure that children do not grow up as homosexuals. These are listed in the Sex Information and Education Council of the United States Study Guide on *Homosexuality:* "(1) Creating a climate of opinion that will allow homosexuality to be openly and reasonably discussed and objectively handled; (2) providing for adequate sex education of both parents and children, so the homosexual can understand himself better and the community can free itself of its punitive attitude toward all sexuality; (3) increasing efforts to provide family counseling and child guidance services designed not only to promote healthy family life but also to provide specific help for parents whose children show early signs of developmental difficulties, before these become fixed." Some say unless there is a change in attitude toward homosexuality, that its practice will continue to flourish.

The overt homosexual has not been well accepted by society. He is still the subject of jokes, punishment, exclusion, and persecution. As a result, some homosexuals have organized homophile organizations to improve the social position of the homosexual, to promote a better public image, and to improve his or her legal status. The most noted of these organizations are the Mattachine Society and the Daughters of Bilitis. What do the homosexuals want? R. E. Masters, in his book, *The Homosexual Revolution*, summarizes some of the demands by the homosexuals. The following demands are quoted from *Counseling the Invert* by John Cavanaugh, M.D.:

1) The homosexual, both male and female, wants the right to serve in the armed forces.

2) The homosexual, does not feel he should be excluded from government services for security reasons.

3) Marriages between homosexuals should be legalized and the various consequences of this should follow, such as joint ownership of property and income tax deductions.

4) Married homosexuals should be allowed to adopt children.

5) Realistic presentation of homosexual life should be allowed in movies, in TV, and in literature. Such presentations should be subject only to the good taste applied at présent to heterosexual themes.

6) Homosexual marriage should be accepted by the various religious groups.

7) Homosexuals should be allowed to wear such clothing, makeup, and perfume as their personality dictates.

8) The homosexual press should enjoy the same freedom as that of the heterosexual press in the matter of pinups, etc.

9) Homosexuals should be allowed to display their affection for each other as openly as do heterosexuals within the limits of good taste.

Many of these demands seem abhorrent to people in their present attitude toward homosexuality. It seems unlikely that all of these demands will ever be accepted by society, but the fact that some of them are already accepted means there is a changing attitude toward the problem of homosexuality. Yet, by and large, society has not dealt honestly with the question and its possible solutions.

Modern dating practices

Education is the primary responsibility of the parents and the schools, and the role of each is fairly well defined. However, when it comes to giving knowledge and imparting standards of behavior in regard to dating, especially as it affects sex, there is widespread confusion. Attitudes toward dating practices are different now from what they were when the present generation of parents were adolescents. Such matters are talked about more freely, and much of the rationale behind the dating standards of the fifties and sixties simply does not apply today because both the cultural and behavioral patterns have changed.

The freedom which young people enjoy in and out of the home, together with an extended period of adolescence (ages thirteen to twenty-three or more), has caused a radical change in dating patterns and a consequent change in heterosexual behavior. Without offering any previous preparation or education, our culture has pushed the adolescent too far and too fast into heterosexual relationships. In its wake, these changing dating patterns have brought many problems that the young find difficult to cope with.

Dating patterns and practices among young people have changed over the years. At one end of the scale, the dating age has gone down, and presently one finds dating becoming a common thing among seventh and eighth graders and sometimes earlier. Social "mixers" in the home are used as a starter. These may be followed by group dating in the freshman-sophomore years, or earlier. School dances, parish events, and pizza parties, are all part of the pattern. A boy especially may not feel confident enough to meet a girl on a one-to-one basis; he may feel more comfortable in the crowd. In a crowd one's personality is not on the line, and he can use crowd activities to keep things going. Around age sixteen, earlier for many, especially girls, the teenager gets up enough courage to attract someone from the crowd and to start dating on a one-to-one basis.

A boy and a girl usually start dating by going to the movies together because they don't have to make conversation, or they may double date to share the difficulty of keeping things going. During this period they may also begin to make out; this too relieves them of the necessity of facing each other as persons. For many this period may involve steady dating for a short or long period of time. "Steadies" can usually count the months, days, hours, and minutes of their relationship. At the other end of the scale we find that dating has been extended to around ages twenty to twenty-four or later before marriage is in the offing. In the college years, steady dating may be followed by meaningful relationships, as they are called, or serious dating. Marriage will come for the college male or female from ages twenty-three to twenty-six, somewhat earlier for the non-college person.

While the picture presented here is a general one which certainly does not apply to all, it points up the changing dating pattern — a long period of time, more than ten years.

Is there a natural process of attraction during adolescence? Nature has provided a boy and a girl with a natural *period of latency,* approximately from ages nine to thirteen, to prepare them for puberty. During this period there is a natural lack of interest in the opposite sex. Boys and girls discover themselves and their identities as male or female before they move out to others. This is a period of strong ties in all-boy and all-girl groups, a time when they test their ability to cope with others of their own sex.

This is followed by puberty, when the sex organs become operative and the sex instinct becomes strong. It is not uncommon during this time for the physically advanced to masturbate because of curiosity. Postpuberty is the period during which the boys and girls seek heterosexual relationships. Thus nature provides for a boy and a girl to solve three problems separately: (a) solidification of the ego, (b) direction of the sex instinct, and (c) development of one's relationship with the opposite sex. The process we have described here usually happens to girls about a year or more earlier than for boys.

Our present pattern of dating has thrown all three of these problems at the young at one time. It is no wonder that some solve none of them. Margaret Mead, a noted anthropologist, has shown that the more mature the attitude of a culture toward sex and the more stable the husband-wife relationship, the longer will be the period of latency and the more mature the young. A look at our culture makes us doubt that our society has a mature attitude toward sex. Certainly the high divorce rate brings into question the stability of the husband-wife relationship. If Mead is right, then the period of latency has been considerably shortened in American life. The effect on the young is bound to be harmful. Might not the present immature attitude on sex and love be due to this evolving dating pattern? What are the long-range effects?

Why does the problem exist at all? Whoever is to be blamed, it is not the young; they have been forced into the pattern by pressures in the culture. Though they object and complain vocally, many parents favor early dating. Children, especially the girls, must become popular and achieve social success. Parents have built a society that strongly pressures the young toward early romantic involvement, and this results in competition. Dating often becomes a marriage market. The culture says that lack of popularity equals lack of social success equals failure. The result is that young children, especially girls, are pushed into the dating-mating market early. For many girls popularity depends on boys' asking and marriage depends on takers. Statistically, more than 50 percent of all American women marry at the age of eighteen or earlier. This means that the number of years in which a girl can succeed socially are limited; therefore she has to start dating earlier. Boys go along with this pattern because they can make out like the bigger boys or the romantic types on TV or in the movies. The result is an alarming number of pregnancies during the junior high years.

Very often the general attitude of men towards women reinforces a negative, unhealthy attitude of a girl toward herself. She is expected to conceal all her personal qualities in order not to appear superior to men. She must give a man what he wants, the preferred type, the ingirl. As a member of her sex, she is expected to emphasize her body over her personality. She should represent whatever happens to be selling well in the market place of erotic values. She must imitate the popular type that the boys go after, even though this means being unfaithful to her self. She should not assert her uniqueness as a person. Instead of creating a type, she must be content to represent one. She is expected to give a man what he needs to have, and when they part, they leave empty.

This description may be somewhat harsh, but it points up some prominent attitudes that early dating practices and selection of marriage partners have created. Instead of seeking each other and so finding each other's selves in all their uniqueness and attractiveness, young people have settled for a fiction. In the mutual surrender of love, in the giving and taking between two persons, each unique personality should come into true focus, for each possesses dignity and value in itself.

Besides early dating, there is the practice of steady dating. This is the price that society pays for awakening sexual attraction too soon and for the wrong reasons. Popularity means social success, and this requires competition for status. Instead of competing, some turn to steady dating, which provides for social security and proof of attractiveness — popularity and social success without competing.

Another cause of this practice may be parents' failure to understand youth. Young people often turn to a steady for understanding, a shoulder to cry on, someone who really understands. Other than the possible moral problems — not respecting oneself and the other — steady dating presents social and psychological problems. Dating is a developmental period, a time of discovery of a person and personality. Dating is a time to develop heterosexual relationships in preparation to maturely picking a mate for marriage. It is a time to learn to love, to work through conflicts. To know a particular man or woman, one must get to know many men and women. Social dating is an excellent way for boys and girls to get this knowledge. Society has failed to provide sexual growth and maturity in love; therefore, youth does not understand the responsibilities and commitment which can develop in steady dating. This is not to say that all steady dating is undesirable; for some who are mature enough, steady dating can help build a monogamous attitude and help teach commitment.

One of the major problems created by long dating periods, together with the atmosphere of freedom and permissiveness in which young people date, stems from what is called the *sexual stimulation curve,* which is the progression from *kissing, necking, body caressing, to petting practices.* The problem occurs when the desire of a couple to show affection for each other results in sexual stimulation and arousal. The use of one or more of the practices mentioned above is called making out.

The plea one hears among the young, "How far can I go?" typifies the problem. As most adults know, the sexual stimulation curve is a progressive one. Tonight, holding hands is enough to express affection and to satisfy the demands of the sex instinct. As the relationship grows and both attempt to put more meaning into it, especially with their bodies, they find that holding hands is not enough to satisfy either their intensified emotions or the urgent desires of the sex instinct. They naturally want further exploration and expression, and hence would like to move from holding hands, to a simple good night kiss, to soul kissing, to necking, to petting, to body caressing, to heavy petting, to mutual sex play, and maybe finally to intercourse. The couple may not be ready to handle the responsibilities these actions involve, however.

If left to itself, this exploration will seek climax at the sexual peak: orgasm in sexual intercourse. Therefore, sexual stimulation cannot be left to itself. The sexual drive sets up the conditions for its own gratification — the person does not. To say one can stop it anywhere one pleases is foolishness. The more intimately a person gets involved, the greater sexual involvement is necessary for gratification. Today holding hands may quiet the sex instinct and give pleasure, but tomorrow something more is necessary for satisfaction. Escalation of desire always takes over in those persons who have not found the resources within themselves for controlling this progression.

Knowledge of the responsibility involved in an intimate relationship such as sexual intercourse should be the basis of not going

Obstacles to Growth and Maturity 153

along with the stimulation curve. This knowledge can strengthen each individual's will in making the decision of how far to go.

In the overall picture, kissing, necking, petting, and caressing are considered love play, the period of sexual stimulation and arousal in preparation for the act of sexual intercourse. The purpose of such love play is not only to express one's love for the partner but also to arouse sexual response, as explained earlier. Since so many teenagers ask the question, "How far can I go?" it is probable that the common practice of making out is really love play with or without sexual intercourse. Some argue that these practices are for the sole purpose of showing affection and fostering the relationship. Some others will say that for the modern teenager such practices are common and not a source of arousal in every case. Yet, young people should be made aware of their implications and dangers. For this purpose, some terms will be clarified here.

Soul Kissing is also called french, tongue, or open-mouth kissing, and is passionate and prolonged kissing between a male and female in which there is mutual insertion of the tongue into the mouth of the partner. *Petting* is male-female relationship in which the hand of the male touches, fondles, rubs, or caresses the breasts of the female either over or under the clothes. *Heavy Petting* is male-female relationship in which one or both touch, fondle, rub, or caress the intimate sex organs of the other, either over or under the clothes. *Body Caressing* is male-female relationship in which the body and legs of either or both partners rub or are pressed against the lower part of the other for a considerable time. *Mutual Sex Play* is a male-female relationship in which each performs all those acts on the other that will bring on full arousal whether or not this is followed by orgasm. There is no intercourse. *Sexual Intercourse* occurs only when there is the insertion of the penis in the vagina followed by movements that will bring on orgasm, especially in the male (from *Teen-Age Sex Counselor* by Betty Glassberg, M.D.). To a greater or less degree all or some of these acts are involved in making out.

Such practices are exciting, but one must ask if there are any physical or psychological dangers involved in playing the game of brinkmanship. Sexual stimulation and arousal progressively gets stronger while love matures slowly. If these practices don't stimulate, then what does? What is left? Besides, continual stimulation over a period of time without satisfaction (even to orgasm) can cause physical as well as psychological and spiritual harm. Many of the causes of frigidity in women and impotence in men can be traced to this experience.

Such actions and practices, instead of becoming an expression of love and tenderness, easily descend to the carnal and become anti-sexual. Whether intended or not, the other becomes the object of sexual desires, and the relationship which started out with such great hope turns to selfishness. Certainly a young person gets great pleasure and excitement out of these first experiences of love and sex. It is fun. Could he or she be satisfied with less in a close relationship with the other? Is each willing to take the consequences to self and the partner? Does this action really foster love? Despite one's desire to show affection and love, the couple cannot ignore the question of the rightness or wrongness of what they are doing. Some would say if it doesn't hurt anyone, then it is all right. The morality of any of these acts cannot be judged on this premise because there is a lot more involved here than sex alone; it involves the respect of oneself and of the other.

The whole problem of the *sexual stimulation curve* derives from the fact that sexual stimulation grows faster than love, meaning, and values. It is a principle that the quality of a sexual experience and of love depends on the meaning and values that the two people bring to them. As two people in love move up the stimulation curve, they must stop at each step to see if what they are doing has any meaning and value. "Is what I am doing moral for both of us?" They must evaluate the results and effects of this on both of them. These are hard to predict. They must be able to develop a relationship without harm to either person. Their time together should be a source of growth to them both. If they decide to part, they should be able truthfully to say that they have been good for each other. They have not harmed or hurt each other; they grew and matured as persons.

A phenomenon to be noted about the stimulation curve is the experience of two people at some point on the curve realistically facing up to the fact that they are well on their way to bed with each other. When they come to this realization, they find out that they have put no meaning into what they are doing together. In effect, they start all over holding hands but this time with much deeper meaning. As love deepens, the necessity for proof of this love in passionate physical contact becomes less and develops into signs and simple expressions that convey a wealth of meaning and memories. Thus two persons' physical relationship may go up the stimulation curve many times as their love deepens and as they put meaning into these acts.

The whole danger in the progressive stimulation curve is the tendency of many young people to develop what Peter Bertocci calls a "paper cup morality." When the last drop is drunk, the cup is thrown away. If the only meaning and value that a person has put on sex is pleasure and gratification, then the other person functions as an object to be thrown away once the pleasure is over. When sexual response is left to itself, it follows the mechanics of the progressive stimulation curve. As a result, the body is prepared far in advance of the person's emotional and moral sensitivity. One can't cope with either the effects on oneself or one's partner. The person will always ask the question, "How far can I go?" because he or she never asked the question, "Why did I ever begin?"

For many young people today sex has begun to lose much of its expressive meaning in their lives while at the same time it has increased its power to enslave them. What may be a simple question of petting another's body for fun may develop to the point where one finds that sex is no longer a way of saying something meaningful to another. It has become a way of slavishly conquering another person with whom one has been progressively losing touch as a human being.

There can be long range effects on young men and women who have pre-marital sexual relationships. As human beings, we need signs in life to demonstrate feelings, thoughts, and meaning to others. Even our public institutions abound with special signs that seem to be needed to give meaning to community and national life. For example, a president isn't a president if he or she isn't sworn into office. A band and a parade seem necessary to give importance to a civic celebration. These signs grow out of custom, but people need them. For individuals, there seem to be only a limited number of signs that can be given. The sign that seems to be the sign of highest unity between a man and a woman is sexual intercourse.

Those who have lost this particular meaning of sex have destroyed for themselves the meaning of the only physical sign they will have as married persons to express complete union and total commitment. Many would argue that it's possible to practice casual sex and intellectually reserve meaning for a future sexual relationship in marriage. However, a young person who has psychologically disassociated sex with total commitment has added a new psychological dimension to his or her personality. We can only speculate as to how this will affect that person's future relationship and understanding of sexuality in marriage.

Dating is a *challenge* to *creativity*. Perhaps the situations discussed will lead to new perspectives, so that young people may now see a few more options open to them. One of these options would be a definite interest in getting to know each other better as persons. Dating should be a growing and maturing experience in human relations as well as fun. At some time or other, one might have to determine whether to abandon a particular relationship in order to have the experience of as many different relationships as possible.

Such practices as steady dating can be valuable in testing one's commitment to a person and in developing a monogamous attitude that will be needed later in marriage. One has to decide whether he wants to drop an existing and valuable relationship because he is afraid of falling in love. Thus, on one hand, teenagers need to test their monogamous attitude, and on the other hand, they need the experience of many relationships so that finally they may choose the right partner for marriage.

Conclusion: obstacles to growth and maturity

We have discussed the major obstacles to growth and maturity in sex and sexuality at some length. We took a look at some of the questionable *ideals in contemporary life* such as modern hedonism, the playboy ideal, the new morality and pre-marital sex. Next, we discussed *sexual aberrations* that inhibit sexual growth and maturity such as selfish sex, masturbation, and homosexuality. Finally, we attempted to put *modern dating patterns and practices* into perspective, especially dating as it relates to sex.

What can be concluded from all this? First, there can be no doubt that the quality and kind of life led in America has brought great changes in personal relationships and in the meaning and value put on sex. The change in the structure of American life and culture will continue for a long time at a rather rapid pace. During times of rapid change, it is easy for one to lose the way and get psychologically or morally hung-up. This section attempted to put into focus some of the possible obstacles to normal development in sex and sexuality. As time goes on, many others will appear in our culture. What is necessary is an appreciation of the objective that sex may reach its full potential without getting side-tracked on the less satisfying aspects. What is needed through these changing times is a fresh look at morality so that young people may be able to make valid and moral decisions about their lives.

13

Sex: Some Conclusions

In this section we have attempted to search for meaning in sex and sexuality. We discussed such aspects as the sex instinct in man, the meaning of sex and sexuality as a positive good, the function of the sex organs, sex in its relationship to morality, and the obstacles to growth and maturity in sex and sexuality. It would be wrong to conclude that the search is finished. In reality it has only begun. Hopefully, many new insights have been gained, new paths of action have been opened up to pursue, and new positive ways to express our sex and sexuality have been found.

We have also seen the intimate relationship that sex and sexuality have to both love and marriage. Physiological sexual response is only one dimension of sex. As we saw, sex was easy enough to define but sexuality is harder to pinpoint. It is the aspect of the personality that reflects one's attitude toward people and sex. Sexuality is the quality of living as a sexually motivated person. In love, the body element is not primary: it is not an end in itself but only a means of its expression. A person's body expresses one's character and personality, and one's character and personality expresses the person as a spiritual being. This is one of the basic themes of this book and the one upon which many of the conclusions rest. The spiritual self — the inner core of what one really is — gives shape to one's psychic and physical mode of expression. This is what happens in sex and love.

The body becomes for the lover a symbol for something

behind it which manifests itself in external appearance, often in sex. True love in and for itself however, doesn't need the body for fulfillment, though it does use the body. For the real lover, the physical, sexual relationship is only one means of expression for the spiritual relationship which love really is. As a means of expressing love, sex is a spiritual act. This is what gives sex its human dignity and makes it a positive good. The body of the partner is for the lover the expression of the beloved's spiritual intention. This is why marriage is needed for its complete expression.

In the young, love and sex often appear as a longing for comradeship, tenderness, physical and emotional intimacy, and mutual understanding. This is only the beginning of real sexual striving. A person's sexual development cannot be something apart from his total development. No one can enter a marriage with expectations about love and sex that cannot stand the test of a life together with another. Sex gains meaning when it expresses love. Both sex and love will grow in meaning only when they are invested in marriage and dedicated to building a home in which all value and meaning will be expressed and externalized. Let us now turn our search to the meaning of marriage.

BIBLIOGRAPHY

Bell, Robert R. *Premarital Sex in a Changing Society.* Englewood Cliffs, N.J.: Prentice-Hall, 1966.
Bertocci, Peter A. *Sex, Love and the Person.** New York: Sheed and Ward, 1967.
Blaine, Graham B. *Youth and the Hazards of Affluence.** New York: Harper Colophon Books, 1967. (paperback)
Brecker, Ruth and Edward (ed.). *An Analysis of Human Sexual Response.* New York: New American Library, 1966. (paperback)
Callahan, Sidney Cornelia. *Beyond Birth Control.* New York: Sheed and Ward, 1968. See pages 119-120 on morality of masturbation.
Caprio, Frank S. *Guide to Sexology.* New York: Paperback Library Inc., 1965. (paperback)
_____ . *The Sexually Adequate Male.* New York: The Citadel Press, 1967. (paperback)
Cavanaugh, John R. *Counseling the Invert.* Milwaukee: The Bruce Publishing Co., 1966.
Champlin, Joseph M. *Don't You Really Love Me?** Notre Dame, Ind.: Ave Maria Press, 1968. (paperback)
Curran, Charles. *Christian Morality Today.** Notre Dame, Ind.: Fides Publishing Co., 1966. (paperback)
_____ . "Sexuality and Sin: A Current Appraisal." in Taylor, Michael J., ed. *Sex: Thoughts for Contempory Christians.* New York: Doubleday and Company, 1972. See pages 127-128 on masturbation.
Duvall, Evelyn. *Love and the Facts of Life.** New York: Association Press, 1967.
_____ . *Why Wait 'Till Marriage.** New York: Association Press, 1966.
Frankl, Viktor. *Man's Search for Meaning.** New York: Washington Square Press Inc., 1963. (paperback)
_____ . *The Doctor and the Soul.** New York: Bantam Books, 1967. (paperback)

Gibert, Henri. *Love in Marriage.** New York: Guild Press, 1964. (paperback)

Glassberg, Betty Y. *Teen-age Counselor.** Woodbury, New York: Barron's Educational Series, Inc., 1965. (paperback)

Goodman, Paul. *Growing Up Absurd.** New York: Vintage Books (Random House), 1960. (paperback)

Gordon, Ernest. "The Case for Chastity,"* *Readers' Digest,* January 1968.

Greenblat, Bernard. *A Doctor's Marital Guide for Patients.** Chicago, Ill.: Budlong Press Co., 1967. (pamphlet)

Grunwald, H.A. *Sex in America.* New York: Bantam Books, 1964. (paperback)

Haering, Bernard. *The Law of Christ.* Vols. 1 and 2. Westminster, Md.: Newman Press, 1966.

———. *Morality Is for Persons.* New York: Farrar, Straus, and Giroux, 1971. See pages 141-143 on masturbation.

Hoffer, Eric. *The Ordeal of Change.** New York: Perennial Library (Harper and Row), 1967.

Johnson, Warren R. *Masturbation,** Siecus Study Guide No. 3. New York: Siecus, 1967. (pamphlet)

Levinsohn, Florence. *What Teenagers Want to Know.** Chicago: Budlong Press Co., 1962. (pamphlet)

Mehl, Duane. *Sex and the Silent Revolution.** St. Louis, Mo.: Lutheran Layman's League, 1967. (pamphlet)

McCary, James Leslie. *Human Sexuality.* New York: Van Nostrand Reinhold Co., 1973.

Menninger, Karl. *Whatever Became of Sin?* London: Hawthorne Books, 1973.

Oraison, Marc. *Learning to Love.** Glen Rock, N.J.: Paulist Press, 1964. (paperback)

———. *The Human Mystery of Sexuality.* New York: Sheed and Ward, 1967.

Pomeroy, Wardell and Cornelia V. Cristenson. *Characteristics of Male and Female Sexual Responses,** Siecus Study Guide No. 4. New York: Siecus, 1967. (pamphlet)

Reiss, Ira L. *Premarital Sexual Standards.* * Siecus Study Guide No. 5. New York: Siecus, 1967. (pamphlet)
Rubin, Isadore. *Homosexuality.* * Siecus Study Guide No. 2. New York: Siecus, 1967. (pamphlet)
Ryan, Mary Perkins and John Julian. *Love and Sexuality: A Christian Approach.* New York: Holt, Rinehart, and Winston, 1967. See pages 57-58 on masturbation.
Suenens, Cardinal. *Love and Control.* Westminster, Md.: Newman Press, 1960. (paperback)
Van de Velde, T.H. *Ideal Marriage: Its Physiology and Technique.* New York: Random House, 1965.
Von Hornstein, F.X. and A. Faller. *Sex, Love and Marriage.* * New York: Popular Library, 1964. (paperback)

What Is Marriage for People Today?

14

Marriage: A Discussion of the Question

What is marriage for modern man? The question is significant during these confused times when many institutions are being critically examined. It should be obvious by now that much of what has been said so far about love and sex was directed ultimately to marriage. In the search for meaning in love and sex, reference was continually made to valid expressions of these as found in the lifelong relationship between two people called marriage. It will now be possible to arrive at some meaning in marriage.

Life is a search for peace, happiness, and fulfillment. For most people, life and a search for its meaning are a venture for two. They have decided not to undertake it alone but with a partner. The common experiences in a life together tell a couple whether they are on the right road. They develop signposts along the way — often measured by the hot and cold of love — that help them see growth and progress in their lives together.

For most people there is only one way that leads to peace, happiness, and fulfillment, and that is the way of special, exclusive love. And love is not a happening, technique, knowledge or action; it is an attitude, a disposition, a power of one's innermost being. Love guides not only the will, the understanding, the heart, and the emotions, but the whole of a person — body, mind, and spirit. It is what gives meaning to existence and direction to life; it integrates and harmonizes one's being. Love means willing the good of the other, and most people choose a way of life in which they find peace, happiness, and fulfillment in willing the good to a special person — a wife or a husband in marriage. Whatever else marriage does, it involves the weaving of two lives together through the bond of love. But two people who fall in love do not live in a social vacuum. Their union in marriage constitutes a segment or cell within the whole human family. Thus marriage is also a social institution.

Americans are committed to marriage as an institution. The Census Bureau estimates that well over 90 percent of all Americans get married. Many people just seem to fall into marriage without much thought or planning — it's the thing to do. The culture says that everyone should get married, and most people rarely think of any other alternatives. Secular celibacy for the service of man is not a popular idea. There is still much of the romantic ideal in the thinking on dating, courtship, engagement, and marriage. Young people are directed to marriage from their earliest days. The image of the successful businessman or the effective politician is one of a secure, dedicated, settled family man.

On the other hand, people generally suspect the unmarried man or woman. Somehow he or she must be an irresponsible, insecure, and unsettled person who doesn't want to get tied down. Even parents and friends persist in looking for marriage partners for the family's bachelors and maiden sisters. Often both are the subject of family jokes as well as of family concern. In point of fact, many of these people remain unmarried by their free decision or out of a sense of obligation — to a sick parent, to financial obligations, a career, dedication to service, or to orphaned children.

Popular reaction to unmarried adults indicates that marriage for many Americans is not the choice of a vocation in life but a sort of requirement in a long series of things the culture says one must do to succeed. When one finishes high school or college, the next thing to do is to get a job and settle down in marriage. Do two people who march up the aisle realize the nature of the vows that they are about to make to one another? Are they prepared to assume the mutual obligations that are implied by living a common life together for a lifetime? Are they prepared as persons to commit themselves totally to another? Marriage is this and much more. It means weaving a life together over a lifetime — not one summer but sixty summers together.

These and other questions must be raised in the light of America's high marriage rate and high divorce rate. It is estimated that more than 25 percent of our marriages end up in divorce and that another 25 percent are so unhappy that they should be dissolved. This means that approximately half of American marriages are to some degree or other "on the rocks." No country in the world has such a high marriage or divorce rate. This seems to indicate that many people just shouldn't get married; they do not have the capability or the willingness to live in close intimate union with another person. Undoubtedly it is also true that many people are not given adequate preparation for marriage and its consequent responsibilities. Whatever the situation it is quite clear that our culture is not preparing young people in a realistic way for the tremendous vocation of marriage.

This section will attempt to search for some meaning of marriage. What is marriage for women and men today? More particularly, what is marriage for the modern Christian? How does a person best prepare oneself for such a marriage? What are the factors that contribute to a successful marriage?

The basic concept is that marriage is a community of persons which constitutes the basic social unit of both church and state. After considering marriage as a community, we will search out those things that contribute to the growth and development of this community as well as those things that tend to be destructive of it. From this it may become clear how one best prepares himself or herself to form such a community of persons. In such a limited approach, it will be impossible to discuss all that goes into the making of a marriage — the legal, economic, social, religious, canonical, sexual, and psychological aspects. The emphasis will be on the personal factors essential to a good marriage.

15

What Is Marriage?

Even the casual observer sees changing attitudes in our culture affecting the traditional institution of marriage, the home, and the family. Some changes are subtle, but others are rather blatant. A radical element of society is asking some basic questions that we need to answer: Is marriage as we have known it in the past really necessary? Is it just a public institution that legalizes sex or is it a private matter between two persons or is it a communal institution?

Because many Catholic marriages seem to be in trouble, we ask what does the sacrament add to a marriage? Basic to many of these attitudes is the whole question of total and final commitment to one person that marriage implies. Why should marriage involve unity of persons (the two shall become one flesh: exclusiveness) and indissolubility (until death do us part)? Temporary relationships are becoming more common. Why not live together until such time that it does or doesn't work out? If the situation becomes intolerable, why should two people stay together and make life intolerable for each other and their children?

Added to the confusion is the changing role of the husband and wife in the home. The idea that the husband is the head of the home and the wife is the heart of the home has given way to the concept that husband and wife are equal partners and companions. The husband is more than the breadwinner and authority figure, and the wife is more than the housewife and bearer of children. The roles of man and woman, husband and wife, and father and mother are rapidly changing.

A changing world has also modified the thinking and attitudes toward sex and sexual morality. Today's parents and teachers cannot tell the young the same things they were told a generation ago without perpetuating outmoded knowledge and religious myths. Research scientists, especially the behavioral scientists, have updated knowledge and have dispelled much folklore about sex and sexuality. As a result, there is a more permissive attitude toward sex among a large segment of the population, especially the young. The relaxation of restrictions concerning dating, premarital sex, autoeroticism, marital compatibility, birth control, and abortion is having a significant effect on marriage and family life. How can this be reconciled with traditional Christian teaching about marriage and family?

All these changes prompt us to ask some basic questions: What is marriage? What is marriage supposed to be for a Christian today?

Marriage in general

Marriage is a social institution; it forms the fundamental community of mankind. Two persons of different sex, mutually attracted to each other by the mysterious force of their instinct and love, freely commit themselves totally to each other to form a creative, dynamic unit, a community of persons called a family. This community first orientates itself inward to the family group to insure the happiness of its members. Yet in time its focus becomes broader as it turns itself outward to the whole community of mankind. Marriage is more than companionship or mutual self-fulfillment or rearing children; it is the opportunity for two persons to form and shape a real community according to their own making — with their ideals, principles, and values. In this view the family becomes something from which its members grow out toward the world beyond.

Marriage involves a growing together in which two personalities complete and perfect each other, becoming a dynamic and creative unity. In the complex daily workings of their life together, which involves many other things besides strictly sexual

What Is Marriage?

acts, two people weave a pattern of principles, values, and spiritual life ideals that give meaning to their mutual love and to their life. This does not come about easily, nor without pain and disappointment. Marriage completes the desire for union in love which is creative and self-perpetuating. Though the aim of marriage in general is love in the fullest meaning of the word, it nevertheless remains true that sex in marriage is the particular physical expression of this love. However, neither sex nor procreation is the ultimate factor. Marriage is clearly a particular and privileged form of preparation during life for perfect charity and love.

Marriage is not merely an appendage to love that justifies having sex together, nor is it an institution that happens to make two people legally responsible to each other and to their children. Marriage is a union in which two people take on the challenge of a common life together. Daily interaction at every level of their personalities takes place. It puts love to work — now creating, now re-creating, now redeeming. It takes for granted that human existence is a challenge requiring constant effort. From the first day of a life together, marriage involves emotional commitments and attitudes surprisingly resistant to change or modification. Sometimes the two persons support each other and sometimes repulse each other, sometimes pull together and sometimes pull apart. All these things are found in the lives of married people who are attempting to forge and to share their quest for value and meaning in life.

Essential elements of a marriage: Two things seem essential for two people to lead a common life in marriage — a total commitment to each other and a total self-donation of one to the other.

Marriage is a *total commitment* to another person — the effort of one's life, goals and values, one's body — for a higher good, namely, the formation of a community of persons, the family. A woman and a man brought together in a common life have within themselves the power to create a community, a dynamic unity, for which they are personally responsible. Marriage then commits one person to another to prepare and create in time a community that will hopefully perfect the individuals and ultimately the world.

Marriage is also a *total self-donation* — a mutual and reciprocal giving of one person to another person throughout their lives together. It is growth in love and the mutual development of two individuals. Total self-donation tends to overcome a tendency to selfishness that often comes between two persons who started off their marriage with so many beautiful hopes and dreams.

Ends of marriage: If marriage is the formation of a community of persons whose essential bond of union is love, we can now distinguish the twofold end of marriage: *mutual love* of the spouses and *procreation* or the creation of a family.

Marriage is the *mutual love of the spouses,* and this is the goal of the community acting as individuals. Love leads two people to a free and mutual gift of themselves. Such love grows and develops in such a manner that it pervades the whole of their lives togther. Their love continually proves itself by gentle affection and by generous deeds. It is uniquely expressed and developed through the act of sexual intercourse. This act symbolizes and promotes that mutual self-giving by which the two persons enrich each other's lives and love. Marriage to be sure is not instituted solely for procreation. Rather, as an indissoluble compact between two persons and as a natural community for the rearing of children, marriage demands the mutual love of the spouses as its foundation. This love rightly ordered must grow and ripen. In this view mutual love transcends the purely physical and psychic states of the persons and enters deeply into the human spirit of each. It results in the sharing of everything held in common, a true communion of life in which husband and wife help each other grow so that they may be true witnesses to their children of the meaning of life and love.

In this sense *procreation* is a social goal and a natural or temporal end of marriage. The common life and conjugal love of the spouses are designed for the procreation, rearing, and education of children. However, it is the mutual sharing of love under such conditions that will be advantageous to the child — in other words, responsible parenthood. The mutual love of two persons is the most essential requisite to begetting a new person under conditions most favorable to the child's growth and development.

The child then is living proof and an extension of mutual love of the parents. The child is a new living being who must be incorporated into the family. She or he is a new person who has a destiny to achieve, a potential being who must be prepared for the future, a person who extends the community of mankind. For this beginning and for this development, the parents are responsible. All this is implied in the concept of procreation as one of the ends of marriage. Some parents seem only to populate, while others really enrich creation and mankind.

Marriage is a *public institution* that is protected by church and state. The wedding ceremony is the public declaration of a vow and a legal contract. This vow and contract is a mutual and free pledge between two persons who should know what they are doing and what is involved in marriage. It is social and hence public because it is a joint adherence to an established institution of both church and state. Since it affects the whole society, it is made in public before legitimate witnesses.

The marriage vow and contract are both mutual and reciprocal. They involve mutual marital rights, a sharing of sex. They also imply a mutual training of the sex instinct and its proper orientation in marriage. The importance of this is seen in the fact that the marriage contract is consummated only after the act of sexual intercourse has taken place. Before this the bond of marriage can be voided.

This contract also involves conjugal companionship, the pooling of all human energies possessed by each contracting party. This involves the total person: the intellectual, moral, emotional, and cultural assets, the financial resources — all these are placed at the service of a life in common in which both partners find fulfillment of their respective individual personalities. The essence of the vow and the contract is the totality of reciprocal giving. Its objective is growth in love and the overcoming of selfishness and egoism.

When two people vow their life and love to each other, they are sufficiently confident that the good things and the values that bind them together will overcome their differences and difficulties. The vow fuses their quest for value and meaning in such a way that they will not allow their disagreements and weaknesses to separate them from the central goal of cherishing each other.

This vow and contract are made public in the presence of all whom the couple hold dear and to a representative of the society in which they live. In a real way the marriage ceremony is love becoming strong and mature enough to take a public stand, freely and solemnly. The two persons are saying out loud what they began to say privately when they got serious about each other, when they expressed their affection and promised love and loyalty to each other through sign and gesture, and finally when they got engaged. The public ceremony tells all the world that this couple wants to accept the responsibility for everything that they can possibly possess and share.

Christian marriage

So much of what has been said thus far has considered marriage as a social reality of the human family of mankind. As we know, marriage is also a Christian reality. Since Christ raised marriage to the dignity of a sacrament, Christianity has attempted throughout the ages to preserve its dignity and sanctity against all sorts of attacks. At no time in history has Christian marraige been put to the test as it is today. Controversies over commitment, birth control, divorce, abortion, and sex before and after marriage, have questioned many traditional ideas about Christian marriage.

What then is marriage for a Christian? It is impossible to talk about marriage in isolation apart from the family and its human social dimensions. It is difficult to view any single aspect of marriage without the whole picture, which in the concrete is the family. We have said marriage is a partnership of love and life. This partnership involves as many diverse things as can be included in one's life and love. But for the Christian, this partnership attains its greatest dignity and strength when it is a partnership for mutual salvation, a life project that is proof that the persons truly cherish each other. Out of this grows a deep personal unity which does not remain exclusive but really unites the couple to the whole community of mankind and to God. Thus it realizes the great commandment of Christ — the total love of God and the love of neighbor in the measure that one loves oneself.

The giving up of self-centeredness, moving out to others in love has its meaning in God. This movement to others is also the source of grace. The outpouring of conjugal love finds its first and finest expression in the love of parents for their children. From here love moves to others outside the family circle. Whether we consciously intend it or not, every act of genuine love for another human being is primarily an act of love of God. This essential referral to God is the basis of the ultimate depth of love and grace between two human beings. Through love one achieves his own salvation and works for that of the partner. In such a movement of mutual love both spouses attain God as their salvation. Through human love, God communicates himself to man, and this makes man's love for him and others possible. Therefore, conjugal love implies a unity with all mankind and with God.

For the Christian, marriage is not merely a secular, social institution; it is also a sacrament. When two baptized Christians are bound in a sacrament of matrimony, this ceremony becomes, in fact, a public sign of the inmost personal unity in love between two persons. The personal love within the couple is supported by God's grace, which not only heals selfishness and differences but opens up the depths of love to others and to God. Because Christ raised the human love between husband and wife to the dignity of a sacrament, conjugal love should not be so exclusive that it is closed off from everyone else. Because of its depth and strength, it should open itself to others. The couple are able to love all people in God. Conjugal love, graced by God, is really union with all mankind, which is also moved by God's grace. The family of man is not a group of persons but a unity of individual and unique persons formed by a love that unifies. Conjugal love is then an event of both love and grace which unites one unique individual with another and also unites both with God and man. The implication here is that a marriage will work when the couple make the sacrament operative in their daily lives by the kind of lives they lead. The couple must make it work.

In this way the marriage of two persons is clearly the sign of love expressing the union of God and man. When the marriage of two persons manifests the unifying love of God's grace, marriage becomes a sacramental event of grace. Yet for all this, marriage is truly a mystery, and married people experience its reality according to the measure of their faith and love. In marriage the Church becomes present in the smallest community of redeemed mankind; marriage establishes the smallest church. This may seem ideal, but in the reality of daily living the couple must work at it placing their faith in the help of God.

The sacrament of matrimony is not something magical or automatic; its potential is unbelievable, but it requires effort and good will. God never gives someone a job to do without giving that person the grace to do it. So it is with marriage. The grace of the sacrament is potential, conditioned to the needs, problems, and efforts of the couple. In the concrete, modern married life with its obligations and responsibilities requires a wisdom, a patience, a faith in God that needs the help of grace. At one time conscience was formed by simple reflections on the matter at hand, but today the whole world of opinion and contradiction is there to influence decisions. A person has to decide on one's own position, attitude, and way of doing things. Whether a person likes it or not, she or he must set up personal values and principles and choose a path. Each person remains absolutely and entirely responsible for one's life.

Today more than ever, Christians need the help and grace of the sacrament of marriage to face realistically the problems, duties and responsibilities of married life. The spouses must become for each other mutual instruments of grace, to make it possible for the couple to fulfill their obligations as well as to meet the challenges of their common life together. Their conjugal love becomes the source and instrument of growth and grace. It finds its expression in the physical love of husband and wife as well as in all those large and little things between two people who genuinely love one another.

Conclusion

In this chapter we have considered marriage as a human-divine reality since it touches the couple's relationship to both man and God. As a human reality, marriage is the creation and formation in time of a community of persons whose specific purpose is the fulfilling of both the individuals, the children, and the world. As a Christian reality, marriage is the creation and formation in time of a Christian community whose specific purpose is the eternal salvation of all its members. This partnership is graced by the sacrament of matrimony when the spouses express their unity through their mutual love. While we have discussed these two realities separately for purposes of understanding, they are truly one. All human love where it exists is graced by God. The sacrament of marriage assures us of Christ's presence in the life of people devoted to each other.

16

How Can A Person Best Prepare for Marriage?

At some time or other, a girl or a boy begins to ask questions like: "Should I get married? Do I want to give up my independence and commit myself to another person for life in an intimate relationship?" Perhaps a more basic question that will help answer all others is: "What could I bring to marriage as a person? Will this be enough to sustain a life together with another person?"

By answering this last question truthfully, a person will know how well prepared he or she is for marriage. If positive qualities in one's personality are not very numerous, there is much to do before he or she can seriously consider sharing life with another in marriage. Sex or even love alone can never hold a marriage together if the partners bring very little of themselves into it.

Knowledge of self and others.

So much of the success and failure of marriage depends on what the girl and boy bring to marriage as persons. Marriage is not a cure for basic personal problems, sexual or otherwise. In fact, the intimate life demanded by marriage complicates basic personality problems. Knowledge of self and others, especially of the opposite sex, is necessary for any type of life together with another. It isn't necessary for this self knowledge, however, to be total or complete before marriage — only life itself can place a man or woman in enough day to day situations for that person really to begin to understand self in all its dimensions. What is necessary to complement this self knowledge is a basic acceptance of oneself, a basic sense not only of one's own personal interests, goals and values, but also of one's basic goodness.

In Section One on love we stated that really to love another person one must first be able to stand as an individual, independent person. Yet we've all seen beautiful marriages in which a shy husband or wife seems to flower and develop as a strong person after years of married life. What has taken place? The apparently self-doubting individual has a basic sense of self-respect which has been nurtured and developed by the love and respect given by the stronger partner. The basic qualities for independence were there; a good marriage built and fulfilled the confidence and independence of the partners.

Marriage is the ultimate in sharing, yet one can't share something one doesn't have. A good rule of thumb a young person must ask when approaching marriage is this question: "What am I, what do I have to share? Am I somebody with interests, good qualities and achievements to share? Am I willing to grow so that I can share more?" If sharing and total self-donation are based on self respect, than each partner is free to grow and allow the other to grow as well.

Identity: "Who am I? Who are you?" These questions must be asked by those thinking of marriage. By this time in life, a person should have some concrete answers. Everyone has a set of values that operate in daily life. One is not always conscious of what these values are, but they affect decisions and courses of action. There is a specific value one puts on money, religion, pleasure, work, sex, person, and love. Problems concerning values arise when the values that one holds intellectually are not the values that operate in one's life. People who talk a good game but whose actions reveal a different person really don't know themselves. There is a difference between intellectual values and "gut" values that determine our actions.

If a married couple has an honest relationship, however, there is often hope of changing this approach to life. If one partner begins to sense that they are fooling themselves when it comes to living a certain value, he or she ought not hesitate to begin to discuss this in order somehow to try to change it. The classic example is the mother who, working to provide extra material things for the family, comes to feel that she is unable to give sufficient personal time to her children. She owes it to her husband and herself to take this question seriously and ask, no matter how hard it is to discuss it, "How many of these things that we own do we really need? Are we primarily interested in a good family life?" Perhaps a couple is unable to decide the answers to this kind of self-analysis, but they owe it to each other to make the effort.

The other classic example is the father who involves himself in so many capacities of service to others that he is unable to serve the personal needs of his family. How difficult it is for him to question which values are operating here, or for his wife to ask why he is so busy. If husband and wife respect themselves and each other, however, they will be able to probe these questions together and continue to build a close life together.

In one's growth and self-development as persons, certain virtues seem necessary if one wants to live in the intimate union with another that marriage demands. At the top of the list is the ability to communicate at all levels of human life — physical, psychic, and spiritual. A person must develop the means to communicate one's true self to others — one's values and moral character, thinking and feelings, attitudes and tastes — in a word, all those things that make a person what she or he is.

It's unrealistic to think that a young couple beginning a new life together is totally skilled at communicating how they think, feel, and react. Yet marriage, as we said before, is a mystery, a unique catalyst in human relationships. In paradoxical fashion, a successful marriage promotes better communication between husband and wife; and as better communication is developed, the marriage becomes even more successful.

Let's look at an imaginary couple and describe the type of steps which can occur in their continuing communication. As an engaged couple, they share ideas about their hopes and dreams, their likes and dislikes, and their fears, disappointments, and joys. As a young married couple they communicate about their joys in being married, their plans for establishing home and family and their mutual agreement and disagreements over how this is done. As a couple who begin to advance in years, they must begin to communicate about their development as persons, about their successes and failures, about their roles as parents, lovers, and career persons, about their roles as friends to others, and about their spiritual goals. As a couple who approaches the "empty nest" stage, they must come to accept together what they have accomplished in life, what they demand of themselves in the future, how they want to fill up their time. As a retired couple they must communicate about their peace or dissatisfaction with life and with their children, with their material and spiritual goals, and about their approach to death.

Each of these stages in their lives may present new hurdles to communication, or brings new plateaus of closer unity through speech, attitudes, and feelings. The particular attributes each person has affects how easily he or she can deal with the different stages of life. If the couple is motivated to keep on seeking unity and the happiness of the other person, communication will grow. If either partner becomes "frozen" in a particular stage of marriage, becomes introverted around the needs or fears of self, or becomes hung up on achieving a particular goal, a road-block is thrown into the ability to communicate. If either partner anywhere along the line is afraid to reveal his or her "real" self, for fear of being rejected, communication will cease. If either partner insists on interpreting the words, actions, and habits of the other within the terms of roles learned earlier in childhood — and refuses to remain open to the fact that the loved one doesn't really "mean it the way you think" — communication will cease. If either partner expects the other to have some kind of intuitive knowledge about the innermost thoughts and feelings of the other even though they haven't tried to put those thoughts and feelings into words, communication is going to be hindered.

Each stage of marriage requires new efforts at communication because there are new things to communicate about. Difficulties in understanding each other in new situations need only be minor, however, if the basic disposition has remained the same throughout the marriage: the basic acceptance of each other, the basic willing of happiness towards the other, and the basic trusting commitment of one to the other.

Any kind of communication between persons is strongly affected by one's ability to listen. Most people are poor listeners, and as a result, they cut themselves off from many of the things others are trying to communicate. A spouse who perceives an inability to listen must begin to ask what preoccupations or fears prevent him or her from really listening.

Maturity: By the nature of its obligations and responsibilities, marriage demands a particular kind of maturity. Human personality is always developing, and it must be flexible enough to assume different roles as time or events require. The marriage ceremony does not make a husband or wife, nor does the birth of a child make a father or mother. What, we may ask, are the factors called into play when people develop new roles together? The ideal answer is, "They must work this out together and come to common agreement." But it doesn't always work like that. We see many marriages in which the roles each partner lives don't really jell. We see marriages where couples are openly in disagreement over the choices the other makes in living a role. If we probe deeper into these conflicts, we often find that the respective partners are caught up in the role patterns they as children learned from their parents. Taught from infancy that certain traits or patterns of life style of mother or father are "right" or "wrong," a person has difficulty changing these concepts as an adult. The man who insists that "woman's place is in the home" is merely passing on what he was taught by someone. A woman who believes that the man must make all the major decisions in the home is merely passing on to her children an idea she was taught, but it's not *the* male role that must be lived in the home.

A couple faced with role conflicts have two problems to deal with: first of all, each one must become aware that such attitudes are "learned" and not necessarily "right" or "wrong"; secondly, each partner must feel basically secure if the couple is to successfully create its own roles. The person who becomes rigid in personality development will surely have psychological problems; why he or she becomes rigid in a role is the real question. Which person in a marriage will be able to look objectively at the new life situation and forge out the best role for that particular place in time? The person who is insecure and who has relied on a role to find refuge and reinforcement, will be least able to change and adapt to the needs of the other partner. The inflexible person in a marriage is usually afraid or insecure.

Looking at it from another perspective, we ask, which couple will best be able to choose mutual roles which seem to promote the happiness and fulfillment of each other's personalities? This side of the coin reads in the reverse: the husband and wife who are secure in themselves and in each other, and who trust each other implicitly, will best be able to create together the life style in which they will be truly fulfilled.

Today when the commercial world sells the soft life and the fun life, it becomes difficult to train oneself to healthy psychological, social, and moral habits that will best prepare him for a life together with another. When a person comes out of adolescence, he has definite habit patterns, some good and some bad. They become second nature and are hard to change: some may be irritating habits that will become the source of later marital problems.

It is not always the important things or issues that tear people apart. It is often the small and inconsequential things about another that irritate one the most. Sadly enough, these things are often superficial differences resulting from the person's upbringing. It is usually easier to deal with a person's thinking than with her or his bad habits. If one is in any way sensitive to the way people react, he gets clues now and then as to what these irritating habits are.

Here are some questions a person might ask himself: "Am I

really easy to live with? How do I get along at home? Have I developed strong friendships with people of my own sex? With the opposite sex? Are people attracted to me? Why? Are people repulsed by me? Why? What habits do I have that irritate others? What will I bring to marriage as a person that will probably be a source of problems in a life together with another?'' To be able to answer these questions to some extent is a sign of growth in maturity.

Social Development: Basic to any preparation for marriage is the ability to develop healthy heterosexual relationships. Most of the teenage years are given over to this kind of activity. Every young person wants to test his or her ability to attract members of the opposite sex. All kinds of good and bad things go into this interaction, but every one wants to think that she or he is attractive enough to come into a close relationship with another. For most this development of heterosexual relationships during these years is an exciting time. It is full of infatuations, problems, and difficulties but mostly the fun and excitement of discovery. Love runs the gamut of emotions.

Social dating is the crucible of experience in which true friendships and love grow and are painfully purified. The youthful and infatuating experiences of falling in love begin to blossom into the state of really being in love. Each new experience of another person provides new insights about people, both about others and about oneself. It is a discovery and an education, so that dating becomes a kind of steppingstone to love and eventually to marriage.

Dating tests many things in a young person's life. His attitudes and practices on a date indicate the value that he puts on sex. What is one looking for on a date? Sexual attraction is certainly an important part of social dating, and because of its nature, part of every heterosexual relationship. The important thing is not that the sex drive is present in such relationships, but how the couple deals with the impulses of the sex instinct and sexual desires. As mentioned in Section Two, the sex instinct must be ordered; that is, it must be directed to a loving relationship.

Dating offers the best opportunity to develop the direction and control of the sex instinct. More directly, dating allows a young person to develop a monogamous attitude, the fidelity to one person.

Social dating also tests one's expectations. Through the mass media people are being constantly bombarded with various views of love, sex, and marriage. In a very real sense, people build up expectations of what these things are all about. Many times the reality falls far short of the expectations that people bring to them. This does not mean that the reality lacks something or that it is not good or satisfying. It is only that people have allowed themselves to build up a false picture of the reality so that their expectations are raised beyond the point of ever being satisfied.

Romance cannot continually exist. Conflict, frustration, anger, alienation are part of most human relationships, especially where there is meaningful intimacy. There must be understanding, forgiveness, self-examination, reconciliation, openness, and confession. Part of loving a wife or a husband is allowing her or him to be human, to have moments of impatience, selfishness, or thoughtlessness. One cannot always expect to be cherished and loved, and expectations must fit reality. They cannot give what they don't have; they can only give themselves. Because marriage is a special kind of intimate human relationship, it should be approached realistically: there will be wonderfully good days, difficult days, and unhappy days in every marriage.

Immediate preparation: A decision to marry

In the back of the minds of most young people is the desire to get married, but the desire to marry is miles away from the actual decision to marry. To the teenager, dating is for fun rather than for any kind of meaningful preparation for marriage, remote or otherwise. While it is true that some people seem just to drift into marriage and others go in blindly, there are many others who decide to get married after mature consideration.

Courtship: There comes a time when a young woman and a

young man, after mature consideration of themselves, their possibilities as persons, their strengths and weaknesses, decide on marriage as a vocation in life. In such a decision, each person wants to share not only one's life but one's whole person with another. The person feels that he or she has the capacity to love, the desire and generosity to give and share, the willingness to donate oneself to another, and the strength of character to commit one's person totally to another for a lifetime.

This decision to marry could be independent of any particular person at the time. This presupposes that dating has been a real part of the person's life. In fact, the decision may be more valid if one is not emotionally or otherwise involved. At this time, social dating becomes more selective than before. Dates are evaluated as social companions. If one has learned anything from past adolescent experiences, he or she will be able to evaluate self in relationship to others. The intelligent selection of a marriage partner is not based upon love or sex alone but on all those things that go to make up a successful life together — social, psychological, cultural, moral, and religious.

When a person has made the decision to marry, she or he can test a readiness to marry. True love wants to prove itself. Hasty decisions during this time will only lead to trouble later. Differences should be exposed, known, and worked out before, not after. Infatuation, exaggerated romanticism, strong emotionalism, impetuous physical demands — all these belong to young puppy love, not to the love of a mature person seeking a marriage partner.

This is also a time to test attitudes, values, ideals, and personality. The ability to solve conflicts and differences is a sign of growth in love. Two people who sweep their problems and troubles under a rug hoping they will go away are heading for real trouble later on.

Engagement: There comes a time when two persons agree to accept each other as marriage partners and decide to formalize this intention before their friends. This is called the engagement, the *mutual promise* (not a contract or vow) to enter into marriage in the near future. This promise is usually sealed by a ring and a public announcement.

In the light of its dignity, the importance to the individuals involved, the consequences to the children that may be born, and the possible eternal salvation of the spouses and the children, marriage as a vocation must be chosen for the right reasons. Money, social status, sexual passion and desire, necessity resulting from pregnancy, and sympathy should never be among these reasons.

Yet there is no foolproof way in which a person can assure herself or himself of the right mate for marriage. The romantic ideal of song and story that says, "we were made for each other," just doesn't fit the reality. No two people were made for each other. If one's dating and courtship have been serious, honest, and mature, uncomplicated with unusual emotional and sexual problems, true love may well have blossomed with one particular person.

Once two people begin to get serious about each other, they need to re-examine certain areas that will affect their future marital happiness and their common life together. Once love has become fullblown, similarities tend to blind lovers to differences and difficulties. The couple seem to remember only the things they agree on. During the period of engagement, certain areas should be discussed openly and honestly. Some of these follow.

The kind of *personalities* both will bring to marriage is extremely important. This includes their abilities, values, attitudes, habits — all those things that go into the making of a person. Complementary personalities are like gears: the two should know what things in their personalities mesh, as well as what things might be a source of difficulty.

Religion has a great bearing on one's beliefs and practices. Religion is also a source of strong feelings in most people. It permeates one's ideals, values, and attitudes. The religious and moral character of the partners will greatly affect both their lives and those of their children. Outstanding differences in religion can be the source of later marital problems. The priest or the minister should be consulted during this period.

The desire for *children* as well as attitudes toward sex, contraception, and family planning should be thoroughly discussed because they are so intimately related to marital happiness.

The *kind of home* life and life style the partners will plan together is most important. A close look at the partner's present home and home life will be a pretty good indication of what to expect later on. How does he or she treat parents? How does she or he get along with brothers and sisters? How does each get along with the family of the other? Such observations are sometimes helpful in understanding the person. Good marriages tend to perpetuate themselves, as do bad marriages. As the saying goes, when one marries a person, one marries the clan.

Career and finances should be thoroughly reviewed at this time to avoid financial crises in early marriage. Love alone won't pay the bills. In this regard the power structure of the home should be considered. Will the wife need to work? Does the wife plan a career? How does the man feel about this?

Marriage demands great *physical and psychological resources* in both partners. The physical and mental health of both partners is necessary for the performance of the functions of wife-mother and husband-father. This reality should never be passed over lightly in marriage preparations. For this reason, the doctor should be consulted during this period if there appear to be any problems in these areas.

Because of its exclusiveness, intensity, intimacy, and the great amount of time spent in each other's company, the engagement period can cause problems, especially sexual ones. The question of how much affection is necessary during this period is vital. It would seem that the freedom of decision that is absolutely necessary for the courtship and engagement periods should not be complicated by a pregnancy. This factor alone seems to force a decision for marriage, no matter what may be the intentions of the two persons involved.

A chaste courtship and engagement will be positive proof of

one's right intentions, one's growth in sex and love, and one's ability at self-mastery so necessary in later married life. Engaged couples should do nothing that will force the marriage or that could come between them after the marriage. This does mean that they have to deal with their sexual urges or their mutual desire to show affection. Difficulties in these areas will arise and should be dealth with openly and honestly. What do the two people really want? Other areas of mutual discovery besides sex should be allowed to blossom and grow so that undue attention will not always be focused on the physical signs of affection. In this way, the partners will get to know each other better and have a better chance to foster an enduring companionship which genuine love assures. Talking things out will tend to release the tensions that such an intimate relationship can build up.

Conclusion

As a vocation marriage has to be understood for what it is and then chosen as a way of life after mature consideration. We have discussed some of the things that go into preparing oneself for the vocation of marriage. In most cases, these are the same things that go into the making of a mature man or woman. They are all the human realities that we call maturity or adulthood. Because of marriage's awesome obligations and responsibilities in our modern world, young people should not approach this vocation lightly.

We discussed remote preparations for marriage, corresponding more or less to the teenage years. Here we singled out identity (knowledge of and respect for self and others), maturity, and social development as the main factors in such a preparation. We then turned our attention to the immediate preparations for marriage, corresponding more or less to the late teens or early twenties for most Americans, to courtship and engagement as times of testing and decision-making about many things involving the meaning of marriage today.

17

Factors Contributing to a Successful Marriage

Earlier in the section we indicated that more than 90 percent of all Americans get married. Of this number, over one quarter end up in divorce and another quarter are unhappy. This means that about one-half of American marriages are actually successful. These alarming statistics have prompted many groups dealing with family life to study the problem. Why do some marriages succeed and others fail? With amazing regularity, the same reasons seem to surface. In the next two chapters, we will attempt to answer the question according to the best data available.

First, we will consider the factors that seem to contribute to a successful marriage. These will be discussed under five general aspects that relate to the very core of marriage: a good beginning, the growth of mutual love, the development of a healthy and creative sex life, a proper understanding of responsible parenthood, the acceptance of the responsibilities of marriage. In the discussion, we will attempt to specify some of the concrete things observed in successful marriages.

In the next chapter we will consider factors that seem destructive. None of the factors in either the successful or unsuccessful marriage operate in isolation but in combination. In fact, some marriages exhibit factors of both the successful and unsuccessful marriage. All that can be said is that when one finds a successful or unsuccessful marriage, most or all of the factors discussed here are present to some degree. No one can predict whether a marriage will succeed because this depends upon the motivation, effort, and good will of the two persons involved. By considering these positive and negative factors, we may gain perspective into what goes into the making of a good marriage.

Successful marriages need a good beginning

As with so many other good things in life, marriage needs a good beginning. This is assured if the partners have adequately prepared themselves for marriage. Whatever else the beginning of a life together in marriage may be for two people, it is certainly a period of mutual adjustment to living a common life — a life that requires an intimacy in all areas implied by living in close union with another. Such intimacy is bound to be a source of mutual discovery. It will be a time of joys, delights, surprises, embarrassments and, possibly, misunderstandings. For any marriage to succeed, it is necessary that it begin well, even in this period of mutual discovery.

Honeymoon and early adjustment: The first period of mutual adjustment is the honeymoon. It is not just a sightseeing jaunt or a vacation, but a quiet restful period of mutual discovery and openness to each other on an intimate basis. It is a time of transition from the engagement to marriage during which the initial patterns of intimacy and interaction between the two persons are set up. Lifelong habits will have to give way to a life in common, and this could be a source of difficulty. Adjustment in all phases of life will have to be made to get the marriage off to a good start. This can be done if the persons realize that they can be themselves and still be loved. If the couple have honestly and openly prepared themselves for marriage, they should be able to be relaxed and at ease with each other on the honeymoon.

Generally a woman's sexual awakening is gradual — a man's is more impetuous. Both husband and wife must be attentive to what pleases the other. Through patience and self mastery, each must respect the modesty, feelings and attitudes of the other. On the honeymoon the husband may have to break the hymen (maidenhead), the thin membrane that partially closes the opening to the vagina. Although this membrane is sometimes thought of as a symbol of virginity, it can be broken in childhood and not through sexual activities. Opening the sexual passage should not cause any problems, but it should never be forced; the woman's physician can advise her about this before the wedding.

Today's preparations are so hectic, and the wedding ceremony puts so much pressure on the couple that the wedding night could be a disappointment. This is especially true if the expectations of the couple are high. This situation can be dispelled by good humor and patience, by learning to laugh at embarrassing or incongruous events. Further, if the couple take a trip to unfamiliar surroundings, this, added to the natural tension and exhaustion of the day, may make the first night difficult for both. The first sexual experience should be postponed until both feel relaxed and natural. Many people suggest that the couple spend their first night in their new home in familiar surroundings. If they have spent time decorating and planning it, the home would be a natural place for their first sexual intimacies. In any case, the pattern of life together set up in these first few weeks is important for the rest of the marriage.

The first years of married life are a mutual education: Marriage is a continuing education. When education stops, so does growth in all areas of life. The couple must learn to be flexible enough to adjust to growth in all areas of their life together. This must be done together or else the differences that separate them will tend to create gaps that will force them apart.

Marriage is a creative event. Both husband and wife are responsible in helping the marriage succeed. It is sad indeed to see two young people who started their marriage with enthusiasm and love drift into a settled or expected pattern during the first year of marriage. Before love really got a chance to grow, selfishness and mediocrity have already made inroads.

It is necessary for the couple to establish healthy habits early in marriage. Habit formation often occurs naturally and easily, but the process should be reviewed periodically. Most important in this regard are good psychological habits that tend to foster love and union. In addition, the couple must establish a value system that will foster union and develop a happy community. Values are strong motivational factors in the religious, social, moral, and sexual areas of life.

During the first year of marriage, sexual adjustment and mutual sexual harmony take time and patience. For many, sexual awakening is a slow process, yet each partner must come to respect the sexual needs and methods of satisfaction of the other. In the first place, they must come to know what these needs and demands are. This won't come from a book on sex. Sexual harmony requires both knowledge and effort. It is a mutual learning process of response to each other's sexual needs.

The couple should not let their sex life fall into a monotonous routine. This is the time for discovery of the other's body and its responses to sexual stimulation. Experimentation and variation will assure a creative sex life together that will grow as the years unfold. Each act of sexual intercourse will say more and more. Sexual satisfaction will grow as love grows. The physical aspects of sex are enhanced by the psychic and spiritual; if love dies, so will sex, and vice versa.

The most important aspect of the first year of marriage is establishing a home, a community concerned for its members and for the world. The home is, or should be, the secure place where parents and children work out some of the central meanings of their lives. If the home is based largely on economic, social, and biological status, it is built on shifting sand. However, if a home is built on the free hopes and dreams of two persons and their vow to be responsible for each other's creative welfare, then its foundations are as strong as human motivation, strengthened by the grace of God, can make them. Such a home will be based solidly on real human needs and accomplishments.

The establishment of a home is not automatic; it just doesn't happen or follow after marriage. A happy home is built on the mutual adjustments made by the couple in every phase of married life. This requires sacrifice and a great deal of unselfishness. The reality of marriage is different from the romantic ideal which the couple may have envisioned before marriage. Experience is often a tough teacher. The early years of marriage can be happy ones, but they do demand that the partners really get to know each other in all aspects of their personalities and character. Patience, humility, unselfishness, and love will be the special virtues needed for its demands. There can be no rigid ideas about husband's duties or wife's duties in the making of a home. The family is the primary concern for both husband and wife as they work out their future together. The home gives love and sex the opportunity to demonstrate and reinforce love. It helps the couple to sift a worthwhile ideal from a mere dream.

Successful marriage implies growth of love

In the earlier part of this section, we saw that the meanings of marriage are mutual love and procreation. Because of the structure of human life, there exists a unity between love and procreation in human sexuality. Love is the mysterious source of energy that gives the family unit vitality, while sex is the most intimate, physical expression of this love, its symbol and seal. And love is represented by children as the natural yet marvelous fruit of physical unity. Let us now consider some of the practical things that are implied in mutual love between the partners in marriage.

Mutual love implies the ability of two persons to understand and to accept the fundamental differences between men and women. Mutuality and unity — the basis of a successful marriage — must be created from these differences in such a way that neither person will lose his or her unique identity. Neither person should "give up everything" to promote the other's happiness. The ability to relate, to discover the inner being of the other, is basic to a happy marriage. Men and women complement one another in many areas of life, such as age, education, religion, economic and social background, upbringing and type of family life. In such complementation, there are dynamic forces at work that express themselves outwardly in needs and feelings.

Human relationships need to be satisfied and not thwarted. Therefore continued growth in all the qualities of mature love, combined with a sense of sacrifice, understanding, patience, tolerance, is essential to the success of marriage. All men and women have some psychological as well as physical needs that must be satisfied, but they differ in intensity. One person may especially need demonstrations of esteem and admiration; another may need to be listened to and reassured; another may especially need physical demonstrations of love, or especially need to be touched and caressed; another may especially need to be one who serves, aids, and consoles the other. Certainly one of the things that drew them first together was this satisfaction of needs and feelings. This should continue in marriage.

Mutual love implies that one know the other person well enough that one's expectations of them are realistic. A person should not enter marriage with assumptions about a common life together or about the making of a home that cannot stand the test of an intimate life together. If the initial love of the two partners built its foundations only on financial stability and assured social success without looking into basic values and capabilities, it is doomed to fail. Mutual love needs to develop new dimensions and other values required to shape two lives together, to bring up children, and to create a home that is alive and vibrant.

What do each of the spouses expect of each other as companions, wife or husband and father or mother? For expectations to be realistic, they should be based upon practical considerations. Because of the changing views of the place of men and women in American society, role expectation could be a problem to some. The women's liberation movement will have an increasing impact on this. What is important is the unity of the family — that things must be done not for one or the other of the partners alone but for all. On the other hand, husband and wife should each be able to find individual fulfillment, not personal annihilation. The challenge of future marriages will hinge more and more on this point.

Within the context of the economy, couples will need to walk a balancing act on the fine line between personal fulfillment and obligation to family and to one another.

Mutual love implies an ability to communicate, to open the door of one's personality and inner self to another. This means the ability to solve conflicts and problems as they arise plus an openness and honesty in both husband and wife in all matters of family concern. These are the ingredients of a happy and successful marriage. The partners must continually work at improving communication; it doesn't just happen. Communication is more effective if the spouses realize that each brings knowledge as well as emotions and feelings to the communication. In so many instances, feelings and emotions take over before facts and understanding enter the picture. Realistic solutions can come once the emotions have been accepted for what they are and understandings reached.

In this regard, handling of tensions is a key to success. The wife and husband should never let each other get to the end of his or her tolerance level where one can't stand it any more. Most frustration is not bad; it can strengthen character and stimulate growth. But frustration unresolved or repressed for prolonged periods of time tends to be destructive, especially if it leads to neurotic or psychotic tendencies. Conflicts, arguments, sexual difficulties, unhappiness, or setbacks in the home are sure to bring about tensions in marriage, but good communication can easily defuse the situation. A good rule of thumb is *Never let the sun set on an argument or a problem that needs solving.*

Mutual love implies the ability to give and to share. Marriage is an honest and total donation of self upon which the unity of the whole family depends. The emphasis here is on total. One often hears that marriage is a fifty-fifty proposition between husband and wife: Give fifty percent and get fifty percent in return. This sounds like a business deal, not a partnership of love. This is not surprising because, like everything else, people tend to turn marriage into a commodity. A fifty-fifty proposition is headed for trouble because no one can maintain this constant level throughout a lifetime.

What happens when one or both of the partners sink below the 50 percent mark? What holds the marriage together then? Total commitment and total self-donation mean that one gives 100 percent of oneself to another. There may be times when one doesn't get anything in return. When this giving and sharing is total, the marriage is bound to succeed despite all its ups and downs.

Of themselves, each of the partners is incomplete and therefore must effect a oneness, a unity. The two must become one flesh. Because all of us are unique individuals, no two people can agree on everything. If they could, life would be terribly dull. Differences, honestly faced and accepted, lead to stimulation, growth, initiative, and creativity. How can two unique personalities achieve a oneness, a unity demanded by a good marriage? If the couple learn how to give and share in all areas of life — work, play, religion, love, sex, and all the other things that make up a life together — they will create a oneness that will stand the test of time and conflict. The result will be a solidarity and a sense of togetherness that will forge a unity.

Successful marriage implies healthy sex life

Reproduction has less to do with the meaning of living than it has with the meaning of life. Instinctual gratification and biological reproduction are only two aspects of marriage and not the most important ones. The spiritual factor of love is the more essential. Marriage joins two lives together, not simply in the sexual experience of intercourse, but in that giving and sharing that only marriage and dedication to a home make possible. Despite all the ideals that we may set for sex and love in marriage, it is many things to the two people in the human situation of daily living together.

To think that every act of sexual intercourse must be solely an expression of love would be to deny the reality and experience of people. At times sex may simply express a release of tension, intense passion, aggression, pleasure for pleasure's sake, frustration, or even hate or hurt. But the meaning of sex is to foster growth and mutual love; the partners should always direct it to these ends. Sex and sexuality should be no more sacred and mysterious than the rest of human life. Yet it does demand respect and dignity because of its connection with love and with the creation of new life. The body is good, sex is good, and both should be accepted and enjoyed to the fullest by both partners in marriage.

Meaning of sex for the married: Conjugal love aspires to a union which extends much further than that of simple friendship or parental love. It desires bodily union in sexual intercourse as a specific fulfillment of total union; it is unique, deep, mutual self-donation. For the lover, union with the beloved in sex is desired above all; pleasure is only the reward. All the ecstasy possible in sex is linked to this union with the beloved. By its nature, sex is never neutral. It affects the two persons involved. To neutralize sex means to miss it, to deprive it of all possible significance for human happiness. It is to reduce sex to the animal level. To be the ultimate expression of conjugal love and the perfect fulfillment of union, sex must be appreciated in its totality — the physical, the psychic, and the spiritual.

Sex is an expression of the deep mutual love of the spouses. It is also by its nature procreative. Children are the living, marvelous expression of love and the bond that can help it grow. The meaning of the bodily union in sexual intercourse is extended when we realize that the same act which is the expression of mutual self-donation and fulfillment is also a source of a new human being. Acts of sexual intercourse that are procreative can be special in the lives of husband and wife. There is a unity between love and procreation, and this belongs to the structure of human life. In any discussion on birth control, this principle must be considered.

Sex life in marriage: Sometimes the sexual response of either partner leaves much to be desired. The number and type of sexual activities between husband and wife should be such that they foster the deepest kind of communication in love. This kind of union will only come about gradually, requiring as it does patience, creativity, and experience. Some people naturally are insensitive to the sexual needs of their partner, and only direct discussion can alert them to ways they should change.

There is no part of the body that is bad or dirty. In all things sexual, however, the feelings, desires, sensitivity, modesty, and upbringing of the other partner must be considered. Barriers and puritanical ideas and attitudes are removed only gradually. The wife who was taught as a child that sex is wrong, may require great patience and understanding from a husband who wants to help her. For many people, it is impossible to totally overcome childhood impressions. Sex is one of the important ways a person knows oneself and communicates this to others. For this reason, it is important that one's sexuality does not contradict himself or misrepresent himself to others. Sexual expression can never be isolated from the whole personality because it is an integral part of it.

Developing a creative sex life between two people requires both knowledge of sex and continued effort. What should a husband know about his wife? He should be fully aware of the physical and psychological aspects of menstruation, menopause, sexual response, pregnancy, gestation, birth, and the elements of child care. He should be sensitive to his wife's sexual feelings and needs; at times he should ask her about them. She should realize he can't know all about her physical system by some intuitive knowledge.

What should a wife know about her husband? She should be aware of the nature of the physical and psychological aspects of her husband's sex instinct. She should come to know what sex means to her husband by talking with him and asking any questions she has. If the couple develop a healthy and creative sex life together, they can enjoy sexual relations into old age. The stumbling blocks to this process are monotony and routine.

Some people may fail to realize that there is chastity in as well as out of marriage. We defined chastity as the purposeful control of the sex instinct according to one's state in life. The man and woman should be masters of themselves in the sexual situation. Such sexual control is especially necessary in the early years of marriage when both partners are learning to respond sexually to each other. But this is true throughout the marriage, at such times as after the birth of a child and during periods of absence or illness. Sexual growth requires such control. Sexual harmony and mutual sexual growth are ideals that must be worked for. Mutual sexual satisfaction as an expression of love and union doesn't happen automatically.

Successful marriage requires responsible parenthood

Sex in marriage must also be considered in the context of love and responsible parenthood. The statement of Vatican II makes this clear: "Parents should regard as their proper mission the task of transmitting human life and educating those to whom it has been transmitted.... They will take into account their own welfare and that of their children, those already born and those which may be foreseen. For their accounting, they will reckon with both the material and spiritual conditions of the times as well as their state in life. Finally, they will consult the interests of the family group, of temporal society, and of the Church herself" (*Constitution on the Church*). This is what is meant by responsible parenthood, not only procreation but also family planning, the rearing and education of children. As there is an inseparable unity between mutual love and procreation (the ends of marriage), this unity should lead the spouses to responsible parenthood.

Just as not every sexual act of intercourse is an expression of mutual love, neither does every such act result in pregnancy. Since both wife and husband are charged with the responsibility of rearing and educating their children, procreation should not be left to mere chance. Their obligation to the children is a serious one.

The family and responsible parenthood: The home is an institution rooted in the love that husband and wife feel for each other and controlled by their commitment to the growth of each member of the family in the light of individual needs and abilities.

In the fullest meaning, a home is a moral structure built upon the quest of the spouses for values that can be achieved together and shared with their children, who one day will enter a larger society as independent persons. The home provides the conditions in which all members of the family can bring to fruition their potential as persons. The home starts when husband and wife forge their values together. These are tested and modified, particularly when children begin to play their part in determining what a family can become. Hence, essential to a home is the willingness of its members to share in the quest for values. All this seems to be implied in the concept of responsible parenthood.

Family planning: Responsible parenthood means that family planning is not only advisable but necessary. And family planning means not only limiting the number of children but also spacing the births of the children. Studies of American family life reveal some interesting statistics. The average family size is less than three children, and this number is decreasing. Most Americans marry early and have all their children within the first seven years of married life, usually close together. By the time the parents are in their late twenties or early thirties, all the children are in school. At this time, the mother may go out to work. When the parents are in their late forties (about half of their married life), all the children are out of high school and probably out of the home. Wife and husband now live alone for half or more of their married life.

The divorce rate is high among people in their forties because the couple are suddenly faced again with each other as persons. All the problems they put aside while spending much time and energy raising the family now come to them in all their force. They perhaps spent too little time on each other. This situation will be discussed further after we have given some attention to the family in its growing stages.

The change of attitude toward family planning is the result of many factors in our changing world society. Despite all the arguments to the contrary, people cannot ignore the world population crisis. As medical science improves, the situation will worsen before it improves. Family planning becomes ever more necessary. Increasingly more people are living in urban or suburban areas of the country. The responsibility of raising a family in such an environment is difficult at best. In the past children were a financial asset, but today a large family is a financial liability. The cost of bringing a child into the world — feeding, clothing, and educating him or her — is phenomenal. On the other hand, recent developments in morality with the emphasis on the person have brought about a change in attitudes and practices, so that Christians today are faced with the problem of family planning and how to go about it.

The confusion results, not from the principle that a family should be wisely planned to insure the maximum of success and happiness to the new community, but on *how* this is to be accomplished to the satisfaction of both partners. The methods of birth control are the central issue.

Pope Paul VI in his encyclical on birth control *(Humanae Vitae)* reaffirms the earlier position of Pope Pius XII that every act of sexual intercourse must be an expression of love and be open to procreation. Therefore, all forms of *artificial* birth control are contrary to the order of nature and hence are an unqualified evil. In effect, he is saying that the *only methods* of family planning open to Catholics are the *natural* methods of abstinence, rhythm, thermal, and other new experimental methods now being developed and accepted. He says that all artificial and unnatural methods are forbidden. Though he said much more in the encyclical and elsewhere since that time, this represents the present position of the Church as expressed by Pope Paul. This position has to do with human wisdom and Church magisterium and must be seriously considered by all Catholics. It is to be understood, however, that the papal position is not of faith nor is it infallible because it does not belong to the substance of divine revelation. It does represent a teaching authority in which the Church is guided by the Holy Spirit. This fact cannot be passed over or ignored by any Catholic.

It is a matter of general knowledge that an appreciable number of Catholics admit that they do not accept Pope Paul's teaching on birth control. For married people this becomes a practical matter of conscience. In several documents Vatican II has repeated the teaching of the Church that every person is bound to follow his conscience "in order that he may come to God," and that everyone will be judged by his conscience. In so serious a matter as considering birth control it is obvious that a person cannot be indifferent. Neither can he or she avoid making a decision by acting according to whim, pleasure, or convenience. If a person is judged by God according to his conscience, it is most urgent that he or she make conscience a true guide: as in all important situations requiring a decision, it is necessary (1) to get the facts, (2) to seek advise, and (3) in relations with God, to use such spiritual means as prayer and the sacraments.

With respect to birth control, the first fact to be considered is the teaching of the Pope. Even though in this case it is not officially rated as infallible, Catholics must accept, in view of his authority, the Pope's teaching that in itself artificial contraception is wrong. A second set of facts would have to be considered by a Catholic couple: everything in their present family situation, such as the size of the family, the ages of the children, the health of the mother and father, their financial condition, and other aspects of their life together. As their decision will be judged by God, the couple will need prayer to him for enlightenment, as well as the advice of a spiritual counselor who knows the teaching of the Church and who is personally acquainted with their personal and family life.

Having done all this, the couple would be in a position to decide if because of some particular circumstances of their family life they would be morally right in not acting in accord with the Pope's teaching at a particular time. They would have arrived at their decision on the basis of a tested conscience.

Birth control methods may be divided into three categories: natural, artificial, and unnatural.

Natural methods: In the natural methods of birth control, sexual intercourse is restricted to the infertile periods of the woman. No drugs or mechanical or chemical devices are used in relation to the act of sexual intercourse. The success of the natural methods depends on the accuracy with which the fertile periods of the woman can be determined. Two ways of doing this are the "calendar rhythm" method developed in 1930 and the new "sympto-thermal" method.

In the calendar rhythm method, which was the first scientific method developed, ovulation is determined from information gathered on *past* menstrual cycles and for this reason is less effective than the more recent methods. The calendar method produces about 14 pregnancies per 100 women using the method for a year. The sympto-thermal system takes into account all *present* signs of fertility in the woman, such as changes in the cervix, mucous and body temperature. Because these are the present signs it produces a 99 percent effective level, that is, only one pregnancy per 100 women using the method. This is comparable to results obtained by the use of the high dosage pill.

The advantages of natural methods are the contentment derived from being able to live in accordance with the Church's directive, the inner strength and spiritual benefits gained from mutual sacrifice and control, and the fact that physically these methods have no harmful side effects. The main difficulty appears to be finding reliable information about their use. Information concerning artificial methods abounds almost everywhere, whereas it is often difficult to find even doctors interested in natural methods. There are presently several publications on these newer methods available (see bibliography).

There seems to be a growing interest among the young in the natural methods as a swing away from being dominated by chemical and mechanical devices.

It is estimated that one-tenth of all women can bear no children and another one-tenth can bear only one child. The natural method is used by many couples to help in planning *to have* children.

Artificial methods: Artificial contraception can be divided into sterilization, which affects the production of either sperm or ova, and interference, which blocks the sperm from reaching the ovum.

The most common sterilization devices are the pill, the IUD (intra-uterine device), and surgery on either the male or female.

The pill *(oral contraceptive)* is a combination of synthetic hormones (progestin and estrogen) which mimics the action of the woman's natural hormones and inhibits ovulation. When no egg is released a woman cannot become pregnant. About 1.4 pregnancies occur in a group of 100 women using the pill for a year. However, for the pill to be effective it must be taken regularly and according to directions. For some women, the pill also has many undesirable and sometimes dangerous side effects. In some women, it can cause sterility.

Intra-uterine devices, small objects (coils, rings, hooks) made of plastic or other materials, are inserted into the uterus of the woman where they spring open. The insertion must be made by a physician. The device may be left in place indefinitely, but it has a tendency to be rejected by the uterus and may slip out. How the device prevents pregnancy is not completely understood. Some believe that the device speeds the descent of the egg so that the sperm cannot fertilize it. Others say the egg reaches the uterus at a time when it cannot nest there because the uterine muscles are trying to abort the device. Because of its low cost, this method is being widely used in underdeveloped countries. It produces about 3.9 pregnancies in 100 women using the device for one year, and has several undesirable, even dangerous, side effects: for example, bleeding and puncturing of the uterus.

The other artificial method is *mechanical or chemical interference* to prevent the sperm from reaching the ovum. The mechanical devices are the diaphragm and the cervical cup for women, the condom (rubber) for men. The diaphragm and cervical cup are hemispherical rubber domes or caps used in combination with a cream or jelly to cover the opening in the cervix, thus providing a barrier to the sperm. They must be fitted by a physician and refitted about every two years or after each pregnancy. Only the diaphragm has wide use in this country. Its use produces about

12 pregnancies per 100 women who use it for a year. The mechanical device for the male is the condom, a thin, strong sheath or cover, made of rubber or similar materials which covers the erect penis down to its root. Condoms prevent the sperm from entering the vagina. Failures occur when the rubber breaks or slips off after climax. Its use produces about 14.9 pregnancies in 100 women per year.

The chemical devices are the vaginal foams, jellies, creams, and douches used to kill the sperm when it is deposited into the vagina. These products are inserted into the vagina to coat the inside surface and the cervical opening to destroy the sperm cells. They are not generally used alone but in combination with other contraceptive devices. When used alone they produce from 30 to 37 pregnancies per 100 women using them for a year.

Unnatural methods: These are called unnatural because the integrity of the act of sexual intercourse is not preserved: The sperm of the male is not deposited in the vagina of the female. The most common means are withdrawal (coitis interruptus), oral (cunnilingus or fellatio) intercourse, and anal intercourse (often called sodomy). In withdrawal, the erect penis is pulled out before ejaculation. In oral intercourse, the mouth of each partner is used on the sex organs of the other (cunnilingus for the male on the female and fellatio for the female on the male). Such intercourse takes place to orgasm. In anal intercourse, the erect penis is inserted into the anus of the female and brought to ejaculation. The methods mentioned here are sometimes used naturally for sexual stimulation or foreplay, but the ejaculation of the male takes place in the vagina of the woman.

Marriage requires acceptance of responsibilities

The success of a marriage depends upon a proper understanding and wholehearted acceptance of the responsibilities of the married state. The couple must know what they are doing. As they are planning a future together, their goals and values should be well defined in terms of themselves, their potential, and the community. Persons who marry being their own unique selves with all their strengths and weaknesses. Their common life together becomes a fortifying spirit of mutual concern and confidence, so that even the greatest trials of life can never destroy their unity, even though at times they might shake it. In getting married, the couple assume duties and responsibilities not only to each other but also to their children.

It is common knowledge that there is no natural method of family planning which enjoys a 100 percent effectiveness level. There is always a slight risk present. Therefore at any given time, a pregnancy could occur. In this event, every mature couple should be prepared to accept the responsibilities of their actions. Contrary to the message we receive from the mass media, an unplanned pregnancy is not the worst thing in the world. As Catholics we have confidence that God gives us the grace to cope successfully with all that happens provided we make the effort. It isn't only the things we plan that bring happiness to our lives. Two people who are dear to each other should not find it hard to cherish a child of their love — even though he arrived unexpectedly.

Duties and responsibilities to each other: Acceptance of the common life and the creation of a community of persons implied by marriage presupposes that both partners also accept the obligations that follow upon such acceptance. Further, the obligations assumed by the couple are mutual.

Traditionally some of the basic responsibilities of the husband are to cherish, respect, and protect his wife; to provide the family with a decent home and a decent way of life; to initiate conditions for mutual growth in sex and love; to help solve difficulties and conflicts as they arise; to help shape a set of values that will encourage growth in the members of the family; and to foster mutual trust, honesty, and openness.

When a man says "I will," he takes a vow. He vows to devote all his assets to the happiness and fulfillment of his wife and children. He also vows himself to the demands of love, day in and day out. A husband's task is not so much to remain faithful even if the bonds of marriage become less attractive but to make sure that they do remain attractive.

Traditionally, some of the basic duties and responsibilities of the wife are to make the house a home for the husband and the children; to cooperate with the husband in all matters that concern the home and the family; to create conditions and initiate responses that will best foster mutual growth in sex and love; to bear and care for the children, especially in the early years; to communicate to the husband the problems growing out of family living; and to contribute to those conditions in which peace, happiness, and fulfillment can prevail. It is the woman's task to interest and involve her husband in the home and in the upbringing of the children. Children need an atmosphere of self-discipline as well as the opportunity to be responsible for their actions and decisions.

Today many would disagree with these descriptions of the role of husband and wife because these roles have changed significantly in recent years. The emphasis has shifted to mutuality and equality with less emphasis on role definition. In practice, each couple should settle upon a relationship that they feel comfortable with and that promotes the establishment of a home and family.

Responsibilities to the children: The basic training and education of children belongs to the parents. While many agencies outside the home help in this process today, the basic responsibility remains with the father and mother. They cannot push it off onto someone else. The tendency of many parents today is to depend too much on such agencies. On their part, some of these agencies, social and religious, seem all too eager and willing to assume obligations that rightly belong in the home. In particular the religious, social, sexual, and psychological development of the child should be of prime concern to parents. In fact, basic attitudes, value systems, and moral outlook will be the product of home life.

Parents must guide, teach, and support their children in the difficult process of striving for maturity and independence. For some families the help of outside agencies (for example, day-care centers) is necessary when the mother works or one parent is not present. Even in ordinary circumstances children may present real problems to their parents during adolescence. Protection and influence often end at the front door. Bringing a child to adulthood requires patience and understanding, but above all constant communication, as he or she strives to become an independent person. More and more outside influences and ideas tend to alienate parent and child. The generation gap becomes real. Parents must take the initiative in trying to understand these influences and keep the lines of communication open.

One source of many difficulties and crises in families today is related to finances and family management. While the husband is usually the main financial support of the family, the management of funds as well as of the home and the children should be a joint effort shared by both wife and husband. Growth in union and love is built upon shared experiences and everyday problems in the home. The tendency in many marriages is to let the husband manage the finances and the wife manage the home and the children.

There is a saying that he who holds the purse strings also holds the power. Finances can determine the power structure of the family. This person can set the goals and ideals of the family and determine who spends what and where. It is difficult to see how such a system of family management can foster any kind of mutual love leading to union that we have discussed in this chapter. Finances and family management should be shared experiences of both husband and wife. It is most important that both know how to handle family assets and run the home. In this way they treat each other as adults and often grow in responsibility simply because they each have been shown respect by the other person.

Conclusion

We have discussed some major factors that can contribute to a successful marriage: a good beginning, growth in mutual love, the development of a healthy and creative sex life, a proper understanding and practice of responsible parenthood, and the acceptance of the duties and responsibilities of marriage. One, all, or a combination of these factors is found in marriages where peace, happiness, and fulfillment prevail. These marriages display a wholesome and dynamic view of life in relation to people and their surroundings. Their goals and values are well defined in terms of themselves and the community. Such families promote an atmosphere of joy, a capacity for human fun and the enjoyment of life. Truly they are good for their members and for the human community.

18

Factors Possibly Destructive of Marriage

To gain some insight into what a life together with another is all about, it is necessary to understand the factors that operate in both successful and unsuccessful marriages. Each sheds light on the other. In the reality of daily living, both constructive and destructive forces may be operating. In any given marriage, not all the constructive forces nor all the destructive forces are at work at any one time. But one destructive factor operating continually over a period of time may break up a marriage. There are danger signals along the way that help indicate trouble.

In this chapter we will discuss the most common factors that can be destructive of a marriage. In recent studies on American family life, these factors were most often cited as causes for family break-ups. We have chosen three basic areas under which many specific causes or factors could be listed: problems arising from failure of the partners to achieve true union; problems arising from early, mixed, or interracial marriages; and problems arising from sex in marriage. Finally, we will consider the dissolution of the marriage by separation, annulment, or divorce. It is to be understood that *anything* that can come between two human beings can also tear them apart, in or out of marriage. The court may give a divorce on the grounds of "mental cruelty," but what constitutes mental cruelty? Or is this just a way of saying these two people shouldn't live together because of other factors?

For the Christian, marriage possesses two fundamentals,

unity and indissolubility. Throughout the book, we have stressed the idea of union in love, sex, and marriage. Unity implies that the two shall become one. Unity also implies commitment: Externally in that the husband and wife live together and share a life, and internally in that they are responsible for each other's growth and discovery. Unity also implies trusting and being faithful in all matters, continually keeping love growing.

Indissolubility means that marriage for a Christian is a mutual and lifelong bond. Stability is the prime requisite for a perfect union, for the fostering of mutual love, and for a normal and healthy atmosphere for child development. The nature of a life together implied by marriage demands indissolubility because marriage involves an unreserved commitment. This indissolubility has meaning, however, only as long as the commitment is possible.

Most of the psychological, sociological, and spiritual evidence to date seems to point to the fact that the union must be an active commitment and trust if such a union is to succeed. The emotional balance, character, and the normal development of children depends on the loving commitment and growing trust of the union of the couple. Parents who love each other in such a union give their child an ideal environment for character building and good psychological adjustment. Love which unites parents eventually fashions from the child an adult who will be well-balanced and well-adjusted. One must admit that many marriages do not achieve this ideal, as evidenced by the large number of divorces and unhappy marriages. This fact suggests that better marriage preparation and post-marriage counseling need to be provided.

One of the most difficult things to accomplish in marriage is achieving a true union between two people in which meanings and values emerge. Shaping two unique and independent persons into a unity in which complementation takes place at all levels of life requires tremendous motivation, much generosity, some pain, and constant good will. Both of the partners must be open and willing to achieve every possible degree of success.

The biggest obstacle to union is *selfishness*. A person may be reluctant to open up and give himself to another. Sometimes this is caused by insecurity, a fear of not being loved. Selfishness may show itself in varied ways, but it comes down to the inability of a person to move out to others. Let us consider some of the ways in which selfishness shows its sadder aspects.

The inability of the partners to solve conflicts and problems is destructive of true union. Some refer to this as incompatibility. This situation arises when the couple are unable to develop meaningful and practical ways of communicating their thoughts and feelings. Channels of communication must be kept open, no matter who has been wronged or what the cost to pride or hurt. Once communication breaks down in any area (social, financial, psychological, sexual, religious, cultural,) or on any problem, the process of isolation takes over. Misunderstandings arise; little by little, trust, respect, and confidence are lost. To succeed in communication takes courage and humility; without these, pride and self pity take over.

Often the partners never really take the time to get to know each other, and sadly enough, don't realize it. In the early years of marriage, they are kept very busy raising children, making a home for themselves and the children, and meeting one financial crisis after another. They can ignore personal differences and issues that really divide them. One of the saddest things that can occur in a marriage is for a couple to find, after their children have grown up, that they really don't know each other. Sometimes people like to sidestep the difficulty by calling themselves incompatible — whatever that means. But most often, so-called incompatibility is the result of human neglect, not nature; it is failing to communicate. Problems must be faced honestly and openly as they arise from day to day. Communication must be an on-going process.

An inability or refusal to focus on the needs of another leading to an eventual loss of love is destructive of true union in marriage. Probably the basic problem here is a lack of understanding of what love means to a marriage. Love that achieves union must be able to overcome the greatest obstacles and difficulties that marriage can present: misunderstandings, monotony, infidelity, alienation, illness — *anything* that can come between two human beings. A couple can allow love to die by not working for a happy relationship. Selfishness and human weakness are always at work. In the first part of the book, we stated that love is an art requiring knowledge and effort. The true test of love is to overcome the monotony and selfishness that can imperceptibly creep into a life together. Growth requires trust in each other, and openness to new experiences, and a desire to create together. Growth requires commitment and determination.

It is a sad thing to see two young people who began marriage with much love and great hopes to allow selfishness, fears, and personal failings to break down their union in love. Little by little they lost what they originally had gained in marriage. Money, success, leisure, social status — too much or too little — are some of the things that preoccupy people and preempt their mutual love.

Redemptive love can save a faltering marriage. In this kind of love, one partner's love is so great that it redeems the other partner's lack of love. The tendency today is to break up the marriage when one person seems to have stopped loving. Redemptive love requires great strength and courage because it requires giving with little or no return. Yet in time patient loving can rekindle love grown lukewarm — it can redeem. Not many are willing to make the effort however; it is easier to break it off.

The inability to accept the responsibilities of marriage also is destructive of true union in marriage. This is a sign of immaturity on the part of one or both partners. Too many people marry for the wrong reasons only to realize later that they were unable or unwilling to accept its obligations. In the light of its dignity, importance to the individuals involved, consequences to the children, and possibly the eternal salvation of the two people, marriage as a vocation must be chosen for the right reasons.

Problems will arise from many areas: finances, careers, family planning, size of family, methods of bringing up children, discipline, family affection and jealousies, areas of responsibilities of father or mother, inability to accept these responsibilities by shoving them off to the other partner. Not to face problems as they arise is a serious comment on the maturity of the individuals involved.

Psychological problems can be another destructive element in marriage. Often these appear as emotional instability or immaturity of one of the partners. Although many of our expectations, needs, and satisfactions are not conscious, they are silently working on us. Festering hopes and expectations are at work on the unconscious level, and people are often unable to express them to one another. No one should enter marriage hoping that it will solve severe personal problems. Such problems, if they exist, should be honestly discussed before marriage so that both partners can work on them. On the other hand, everyone has some personal deficiencies which might be diminished in a loving marriage, such as a social shyness, a sexual self-doubt, or a lack of confidence in one's ability or talents.

As mentioned before, *financial problems* can be destructive to true union in marriage. Financial insecurity and instability are a source of many marital difficulties and more than any other single reason tend to tear the marriage apart. The career demands of the father and the possibility of the mother's working are serious demands that must be examined and evaluated in the light of the life style that family wants to live. For some, status and "keeping up" with others seem more important than a happy home and the proper training and education of the children. Double incomes and double bank accounts can mean double trouble for the family. More commonly today, however, both parents must work to afford the basic necessities. What kind of family life does one want especially in the light of the current economic situation? How does a couple adapt to the demands made on a family by poverty?

Problems arising from early, mixed, and inter-racial marriages

The statement was made that if two people truly love each other, this love can overcome all obstacles that time and conflict can offer. The problem arises when the love is not deep or strong enough to withstand the destructive forces that tend to destroy it. Studies of American family life show that early, mixed, or interracial marriages are obstacles that tend to break up marriages. To succeed, these marriages require extra motivation and effort. Let it be clear what we are saying here. It is not to be implied that these marriages can't succeed. What we are saying is that such marriages contain obstacles that require something extra for them to succeed.

By *early marriage,* we mean principally teenage marriages. Can they succeed in today's society? The chance of success is small indeed. From 70 to 80 percent of all teenage marriages break up within the first or second year of marriage. Statistics on such marriages reveal that most of the brides are pregnant when they walk up the aisle, and the second child comes fast upon the first child. This seems to indicate that most of these couples either were forced to marry or married for the wrong reasons.

There are many things in the society working against such marriages. At the top of the list is money. Marriage, under the best of conditions, is an expensive proposition, especially where there are children. The lack of education of either father or mother, or both, makes it difficult to get adequate jobs in a society where a college degree is often regarded as the ticket to success. Teenagers live on the fringe of the economy, and this is not sufficient to support a family.

Certainly in evaluating the advisability of an early marriage, the maturity of the two individuals must be a prime consideration. Enough factors must be present to insure success. Reasons for marrying must be strong; pregnancy or physical sexual contact should not be among them.

Mixed marriage can be an obstacle to true unity, especially when it involves working out a mutual value system and educating the children. Talking about mixed marriages, most people immediately think of marriage between persons of different religions. Among writers in the field, the tendency today is to extend the idea of mixed marriages to include all kinds of mixtures —

cultural, social, educational, and psychological, as well as religious. Studies show that such mixtures present many common obstacles to a successful marriage, especially if a value system is involved. Since more is known about marriage between persons of mixed religions, let us take a closer look at the problem.

Many believe that only the Catholic Church is opposed to mixed marriages. This is clearly not so. The Catholic Church probably has been the most vocal and insistent but not the strictest. The National Association of Churches (Protestant) has advised against the marriage of persons of mixed religions. The concern is that the earthly happiness and the external salvation both of parents and of children are in jeopardy. Some Protestant and Jewish groups seem also to take a hard line on this issue.

Why are these groups taking the strict view of this issue? Recent studies have shown that an unusually large number of marriages of persons with mixed religion end either in divorce or in the loss of all religion in the family. The ones that do succeed (34 percent) show a strong religious faith in both partners and in the children. Let us clarify a point. When we say mixed marriage, we are not just referring to the marriage of a Catholic with a Protestant or a Jew. The term also includes the marriage of a Baptist with a Lutheran, a Presbyterian with a Methodist, and so on. In other words, Protestant churches tend to be against mixed marriages within Protestant denominations. Further, Jews discourage marriage between members of the different Jewish sects. In the Catholic religion, marriage between a practicing Catholic and a nominal Catholic also presents a problem.

Mixed religious marriages have been tagged as one of the major causes of religious indifference in America. Since such a marriage lacks a common basis for religious ideas, values, purpose, and motivation; it lacks the spiritual resources provided by common worship. One parent must renounce the right to express his own spiritual or moral outlook on such issues as birth control and ideas of right and wrong. This can be a source of conflict and misunderstanding.

To solve the problem of religious differences, many marriages end up with no religion at all. The couple decide to drop any type of external religion from their lives. The children grow up without any religious education or association with any religious group. In cases where the parents take the child to the church of each parent in turn and then ask him to make his own choice, the child usually ends up either totally confused or totally indifferent. It is not right to expect the child to choose the religion of one or the other of his parents. It is better if one parent gives up his right to religious instruction in regard to the children; however, a parent who has strong religious convictions might find this very difficult to accept.

Following the exhortations of Vatican II in the areas of ecumenism and religious freedom, there is more understanding of and respect for partners of mixed marriages. In a mixed marriage involving a Catholic and a non-Catholic Christian, it is the Catholic who is responsible for bringing up the children in the Catholic religion. The only involvement on the part of the other marriage partner is that he or she understands this obligation in the life of the Catholic.

Interracial marriages are becoming more common. The big question is: Are we ready for it? There is nothing wrong with such marriages. But like mixed marriages, there is much ignorance and prejudice on this matter. If we have not come to accept persons of different races as friends and neighbors, it is hardly possible for us to accept interracial marriages. Some people haven't even come to accept marriages among different nationalities, say an Italian with an Irishman. How much less tolerance might be shown then to an interracial marriage? The love of the two persons must be strong enough to bear up under all these obstacles. Further, the children will be placed at a disadvantage. Are the parents willing to face the prejudice and the disadvantages? It would seem so because statistics show that interracial marriages tend to succeed at a better rate than the national average. Maybe they have faced the obstacle before they got married. Maybe they were forced to look at each other as real persons. In the future, these marriages will become more common.

Problems arising from sex in marriage

Most of the problems in marriage arising from sex have been discussed at length in other parts of this book. It is not necessary to repeat the discussion here, but only to review the conclusions. While marriage does present some special problems of its own in the sexual area, often these problems have existed long before the marriage took place. The origin and source may have been in childhood, or in some phase of adolescence. If the personality has grown and matured, so have sex and sexuality.

The major sexual problem is the failure to integrate sex into the totality of one's life. If there is any such thing as sexual incompatibility, it is this — sex has not been ordered. There is a lack of direction and control in the sex instinct. Sex may still basically be used selfishly for one's own pleasure and satisfaction. This is the kind of misuse of sex that will gradually lead to sexual inadequacy and monotony. Such sex needs more and more thrills for satisfaction. It can never really be creative because it is not integrated with love.

In marriage, failure in sex and love is often evidenced by impotence in the husband and frigidity in the wife. The cause of these two problems is almost always psychological and usually symptomatic of some deeper problem. Sometimes sexual immaturity and failure to reach some degree of harmony in sexual matters is caused by poor attitudes and practices. The only solution for the person or persons is to become less self-centered and to learn to face reality. One has to get over the idea that sex is a bedroom fantasy. Mutual sexual response is something that comes with time, patience, and effort and not from the sex organs alone.

Another source of sexual problems is the moral decision to use birth control. In the last chapter, we discussed the birth control issue. We now raise it as an issue that can divide a couple.

The use or non-use of any method of birth control must result from a mutual decision of husband and wife — not from the choice of one or other of the partners alone. This decision must not offend the religious or moral sensibilities of either partner. Responsible parenthood, family planning, and birth control involve not only the number and spacing of the children, the methods to be used, but also the rearing and education of children. All of these can bring about major disagreements between husband and wife.

For some, unwanted pregnancies are ended by an abortion, that is, the interruption and termination of a pregnancy by natural or forced expulsion of a non-viable fetus (one that is unable to survive outside the womb) from the uterus. When the abortion occurs because of illness, accident, or a pathological condition, it is commonly called a miscarriage. Direct or forced abortion is caused when the non-viable fetus is removed by artificial means. A direct abortion may be therapeutic to save the mother's life or health. The safest time for an abortion is within the first three months of pregnancy. The D and C (dilation and curettage) method is most commonly used in which the cervix is dilated by a surgical instrument and the fetus is scraped from the walls of the uterus.

Direct abortion is forbidden by the Catholic Church. Because of the liberalization of laws, the question of abortion is of current importance, religious as well as secular. Presently, the Supreme Court has ruled favorably on abortion. While many states have since passed laws trying to get around the Supreme Court decision, most have been invalidated. While the law stands, anti-abortionists will find it necessary to educate people to the dignity and rights of every human being, born or unborn.

The question to ask is: "What am I really doing?" Is the product of conception a human being from the moment of conception? Is direct abortion always direct killing or murder?" In answering these questions, one is facing the issue at stake: the sanctity of human life as a basic value or good, the inviolability of an individual's life, no matter what he has done or what his condition. For the Christian, human life encompasses more than this present world and hence cannot be measured or seen only in terms of it. Love enables one to promote the total good of the other as a human person, and human life is the most basic human good.

The basic question in the matter of abortion is this: When does human life begin? We can't say life begins at the moment of birth because recent uterine photography shows the baby alive and kicking, even at early stages of pregnancy. Biologists have yet to answer the question of physical life, psychologists have yet to answer the question of psychic life, and theologians have yet to answer the question of spiritual life. We just don't know when the human person begins to exist as a human person after impregnation. Since we don't really know, the Catholic Church holds the position that the human fetus is not to be tampered with at any time. No one but God has the right to deny human life, potential or real, to another. For Catholics, abortion can never be a means for birth control.

Finally, a general cause of the destruction of marriage is the moral decline of one or both of the partners. This may become evident in many ways, the most common being infidelity. Adultery is a terrible wounding of mutual trust and symptomatic of a serious disorder in the marriage. As the partners move away from the ideal of marriage as an expression of mutual love and as marriage gets further away from its sacramental aspect, the marriage will be more subject to destructive forces. The moral decline of one or both partners and the consequent disorder it introduces into their lives will surely bring about the break-up of the marriage.

Separation, annulment, and divorce

The final failure of a marriage is its dissolution by separation, annulment, or civil divorce. Two people come to the point in their marriage where living together has become intolerable. The love that once was a bond of unity has turned to a hate that tears them apart. Up to now, we have considered those factors that led to the breakup of the marriage. Now we need to see the issues involved in the final dissolution of the partnership in separation, annulment, or divorce.

Contemporary America has become increasingly more tolerant of divorce. In fact, the whole question of total commitment to another and the indissolubility of marriage has been brought into question. Most of the fifty states allow a legal separation or divorce for a variety of reasons. Even many Protestant churches approve of divorce in certain circumstances. The Catholic church has held to her traditional position forbidding remarriage after separation, annulment, and divorce, though there are liberalizing trends in certain quarters. Since the family is the basic social unit of both church and state, it is necessary to preserve the integrity of marriage and the family if we want a stable society. There is much confusion on this issue. Today more than ever, it is necessary to understand the issues and what exactly is at stake.

Separation, often called a limited legal divorce, is separation from room and board. A separation can be legalized by the state to protect both partners as well as the children. The separation does not dissolve the marriage, and the couple may go back together at any time. The common life and sexual marital rights are temporarily suspended. There is no time limit put on the separation. For the good of both partners and the children, the Catholic Church allows a separation since it does not dissolve a valid sacramental marriage.

When a marriage begins to fail for one of the reasons we have discussed, it may become necessary for the partners to get away from each other for a period of time to think out their situation. There is not much point to a separation unless both partners intend to work out the problem. In fact, it need not be legalized unless the situation has come to the point where one of the partners or the children are threatened by the relationship. It is important that during this period of physical separation that communication between the two continue. An honest discussion of the problems that made the situation intolerable may lead to its mutual solution. Not talking presumes that nothing can be said.

Annulment is an official declaration that a marriage was null and void from the very beginning — that is, there never was a marriage contract, vow, or sacrament. Both the church and state grant annulments. When the state grants an annulment, it is saying that there was no legal contract, and hence the legal bonds between the two partners did not exist from the beginning. When the Church grants an annulment, it is saying that there was no valid sacramental marriage from the beginning. In both cases the two persons are free to marry again.

An annulment by the Catholic Church is granted by the Church Rota (diocesan or Roman) after examining all evidence that would invalidate the sacrament of marriage. In the past, canon law listed the impediments that blocked a valid marriage. If one could go before the Rota and prove a case, one was granted an annulment. It was a slow process, often lasting for years, yet this is changing. The most frequent problems are a previous marriage invalidating a second marriage or an invalid first marriage that will permit a second marriage. If the church allows an annulment, the couple must go through a legal civil divorce to break the legal contract.

There is evidence that the church is slowly liberalizing her approach to annulments. In the past, annulments were granted only on the strictest objective evidence. It was presumed that if the couple were married by a priest before witnesses, the sacrament was valid.

The latest developments in sacramental theology have given new insights into the nature of sacraments and how they operate in the lives of people. Certain objective conditions and subjective intentions have to be present before the sacrament of marriage becomes effective. In other words, there is more to the validity of the sacrament of marriage than the ceremony itself. In the past it was presumed that the "I do" expressed all the conditions and intentions — the two people knew what the sacrament of marriage was and they knew what they were doing. There is solid evidence that some people who marry don't realize what they are doing, nor do they understand what obligations are imposed on them by a sacramental marriage.

How do we know? The evidence is often clear from the type of life they live together after the marriage ceremony. For example, it is hard to believe that two teenagers who get married in a church ceremony today and who six months later are ready to get a divorce, ever received the sacrament of marriage. In other words, an examination of the married life after the marriage could give positive evidence that the two people never achieved a life together implied by a sacramental marriage. In other words, the sacrament never operated from the very beginning.

Some advocate such practices as allowing persons who are now living in an invalid marriages to receive the sacraments. In the past the couple were considered as living in sin and were denied the sacraments. Today, however, advocates suggest if the couple in an invalid marriage are leading virtuous married lives and there is no scandal involved, they should be able to receive the sacraments. The scandal referred to here would be the adverse effect of such actions on persons who knew their marriage was invalid.

Some people would tend to misinterpret the situation. If the couple had moved to another parish or city where people did not know them or the situation, the public reception of the sacraments would cause no trouble and would be permitted. However, the Vatican has not approved this practice and has specifically condemmed it in some dioceses where it was in practice.

Divorce, often called legal divorce, is a decision made by a judge that a marriage contract is considered by the civil law of the state to be terminated. Legal divorces break the legal contract but not the sacramental bond. In this sense the Church does not recognize a divorce as dissolving a valid sacramental marriage. She does, however, allow Catholics to get a legal divorce to insure the legal protection of the partners and the children. In such cases the Catholic is not free to marry again if the marriage was sacramentally valid. The church's position is based upon the concept of the indissolubility of a valid sacramental marriage.

Since the divorce rate is high in the United States (one divorce for every four marriages), it would be useful at this point to look into reasons why people get divorced. All through this chapter we have discussed things that tend to destroy human relationships. The particular reasons given for legal divorces in the United States are (given in order of incidence): irretrievable breakdown of the marriage relationship, physical or mental cruelty, desertion or abandonment, failure to support, and adultery. The fifty states vary greatly in the reasons they will accept for divorce; some are liberal and some are restrictive.

However, the legal statements are of no help toward understanding the problem because a legal reason does not always reflect reality. Studies reveal the specific causes that lead to break-ups: excessive drinking or alcholism, adultery, irresponsibility, clash of temperaments or incompatibility, in-laws, sexual incompatibility, mental illness, religious or racial differences, money problems. These are listed in order of incidence.

Marriage counselors and psychologists have come to realize that these reasons are really symptomatic of deeper problems. Their experience with married couples point to a number of basic causes leading to divorce.

Emotional immaturity coupled with a lack of self-sacrifice ranks high on the list. Another concerns *difficulties in personality adjustment,* as seen in a sense of frustration and lack of openness. The need for forming a meaningful human relationship was not satisfied. A third cause can be found in the couple's failure to read *the danger signs that appear:* inability to communicate, drinking to excess, difficulty in expressing affection, lack of responsibility or interest in the home, increased faultfinding, inability to enjoy each other's company, indifference to religion or values.

Divorce solves nothing for many couples because the problems lies in the people involved and not in the marriage itself. Often these same people carry the same problems and attitudes into another marriage, only to be faced with the same situations. Studies show that divorced people tend to re-marry with people much like the ones they had married the first time. A far-reaching effect of divorce is that it may leave the children emotionally scarred. In fact, bad marriages tend to reproduce themselves in the children when they later marry.

Not all people should marry. Some people cannot live in an intimate human relationship for a lifetime. This is not to condemn them. Often these single people give up their lives in generous and outstanding service to others. They have deep relationships with other people but not within a marriage relationship. Unfortunately, some areas of American culture do not readily accept the unmarried.

Conclusion

We have discussed some of the things that tend to break up a marriage. Many times selfishness is at the bottom of it all, the inability of one or other of the partners to get out of self and move to the other. Most of the other stated reasons are the multitude of ways in which selfishness expresses itself, always in opposition to the function of marriage as creating and continually re-creating a unity between two unique individuals.

Selfishness is the toughest obstacle to unity. To achieve union is not easy, and for most people this requires a lifetime. There are many things that people can do together that help to shape this unity. For Christians, there is the grace of the sacrament of matrimony that is continuously at work in all areas of family life to strengthen the bond of unity.

19

Marriage: Some Conclusions

In this section, we have tried to search for some meaning in marriage for men and women today, at a time when many traditional views on marriage are being questioned. The family is the basic social unit of both church and state, and when this institution is affected by change, so is the whole fabric of society. As the family is today in the process of evolution, a whole new style of family living is emerging. As in any process of change, some things must go and others remain.

Whatever the changes, marriage as an institution must be preserved as the human-divine reality that it is. The view of love and sex presented in this book demands a kind of union that only marriage can bring to fruition. Even so, there is still a lot of mystery in marriage that only time and a life together will reveal.

In this section we tried to present marriage as the human-divine reality we understand today. We defined marriage as a partnership of life and love in which two persons freely commit themselves to forming a creative, dynamic community of persons, the family. By its nature, marriage demands of the couple a total commitment and a total self-donation for a lifetime. For the Christian, marriage is sacramental and hence a divine reality. Through a life of grace, Christ becomes a real part of the married life of the spouses. In this sense, marriage also becomes a partnership for salvation.

Because of its permanence and sanctity as a vocation in life, marriage should not be entered into lightly. In this section, we discussed the ways in which one could best prepare himself for this lifelong partnership. Those things that go into the making of a mature man or woman are obviously necessary for marriage. Just as people change and grow, marriage can become a deeper, happier union as years go by. The marriage will be no better or worse than what the two people bring to it as persons, but it can become a new, unique thing. What is most important here is that two people who want to marry should know what they are getting into. Marriage demands love and sexuality with all the accompanying responsibilities.

Finally, we discussed the things that result in successful and unsuccessful marriages. In general, whatever makes a loving community work helps a marriage, and whatever impedes community destroys marriage. A creative and successful marriage doesn't just happen; it is the result of motivation, good will, and effort. A marriage succeeds because two people work at putting meaning and value into their lives together.

BIBLIOGRAPHY

Bertocci, Peter A. *The Human Venture in Sex, Love, and Marriage.** New York: Association Press, 1963.
Billings, John J. *The Ovulation Method.* Los Angeles: Borromeo Guild, 1972.
Callahan, Sidney C. *Beyond Birth Control: The Christian Experience of Sex.** New York: Sheed and Ward, 1967.
Christensen, Harold T. *Sex, Science, and Values.* Siecus Guide No. 9. New York: Siecus, 1969. (pamphlet)
Gibert, Henri. *Love in Marriage.** New York: Guild Press, 1964. (paperback)
Gosling, Justin. *Marriage and the Love of God.* New York: Sheed and Ward, 1965.
Haering, Bernard, C.S.S.R. *The Law of Christ.* Vol. 3. Westminster, Md.: Newman Press, 1966.
_____ . *Marriage in the Modern World.* Westminster, Md.: Newman Press, 1965.
Heilly, Alphonse, S.J. *Love and Sacrament.* Notre Dame, Ind.: Fides Publications Inc., 1963. (paperback)
Kanaby, Donald and Helen. *Sex, Fertility, and the Catholic.** New York: Alba House, 1967. (paperback)
Kippley, Sheila and John. *The Art of Natural Family Planning.* Available from the Couple to Couple League, P.O. Box 11084, Cincinnati, Ohio 45211.
Kippley, Sheila. *Breastfeeding and Natural Child Spacing.* New York: Harper and Row, 1974.
Kirkendall, Lester A. and Rubin, Isadore. *Sexuality and the Life Cycle.* Siecus Guide No. 8. New York: Siecus, 1969. (pamphlet)
Kirkendall, Lester A. "Reflections on Sexual Morality." *The Humanist,* Vol. 33, November-December 1972.
Lee, Alfred M. and E.B. *Marriage and the Family.** New York: Barnes and Noble Inc., 2nd edition, 1967. (paperback)
Lepp, Ignace. *The Psychology of Loving.** Baltimore, Md.: Helicon Press, 1963. (paperback)

Marshall, John. *The Infertile Period*. Baltimore: Helicon Press, 1967.

Natural family planning: pamphlets from the National Office of the Couple to Couple League, P.O. Box 11084, Cincinnati, Ohio 45211.

Noonan, John T., Jr. *Contraception: A History of Its Treatment by the Catholic Theologians and Canonists*. New York: New American Library, 1967. (paperback)

O'Callaghan, Denis. "Birth Control Crisis," *The Catholic World*, March 1967, pp. 326-334.

Oraison, Marc. *Man and Wife.** New York: The Macmillan Co., 1958. (paperback)

Rahner, Karl, S.J. "Marriage as a Sacrament," *Theology Digest*, Vol. XVII, Spring, 1969, pp. 4-8.

Reidy, Joseph and Jeanne. *The Risk of Loving.** New York: Herder and Herder, 1968.

Riemer, George R. *Dialog: Dating and Marriage.** New York: Holt, Rinehart and Winston, Inc., 1967. (paperback)

Riker, Charles and Audrey. *Understanding Marriage.** Glen Rock, N.J.: Paulist Press, 1963. (paperback)

Schilebeeckx, E., O.P. *Marriage: Human Reality and Saving Mystery*. New York: Sheed and Ward, 1965.

von Gagern, Frederick. *Difficulties in Married Life.** New York: Paulist Press, 1964. (paperback)

von Hildebrand, Dietrick. *Man and Woman.** Chicago: Franciscan Herald Press, 1965.